Robert Lindsay

Rise Up

Rise Up

This is a work of non-fiction. It reflects the views of the author. Any trademarks, service marks, product names or named features are assumed to be the property of their respective owners, and are used only for reference. There is no implied endorsement if any of these terms or associations is referenced. Except for review purposes, the reproduction of this book in whole or part, electronically or mechanically, including information storage and retrieval systems, except by a reviewer who may quote brief passages for review, constitutes a copyright violation. The last chapter, After the Credits Roll, is a work of fiction. The characters and events in this last chapter, After the Credits Roll, are fictitious. The purpose of the last chapter is to offer an educational entertainment opportunity for consideration to illustrate certain aspect of the topics discussed in the book. Any similarity of characters to real persons, living or dead is coincidental and not intended by the author. To contact the author visit *www.RobertLindsay.org*

Rise Up
Copyright © 2013 Robert Lindsay
Initial Publication, May 2013
Cover Art Designed by Laura Heritage
ISBN 978-0-9894424-0-4 (e-book)
ISBN 978-0-9894424-2-8 (paperback)
ISBN for Executive Decision excerpt 978-0-9894424-1-1
The Library of Congress has cataloged Rise Up 1-964889853

Printed in the United States of America

20% of the Author's profits in 2013 from the sale of **Rise Up** will be split between the *Wounded Warrior Project* and *Fisher House.* Donations by the Author will be made at the end of the 2013 calendar year. For more information on these two great foundations visit their respected websites at: www.woundedwarriorproject.org and www.fisherhouse.org and see how each organization serves our Veterans and their families. Get involved too, as a thank you to those who defend your freedom.

Acknowledgement

To my beautiful wife, Julie, who inspires me and keeps me humble – you are amazing. May our marriage be a light to others and may they be as in love.

To my kids, Sollyn and Kiefer, may each of you discover your passions and gifts. I love each of you in more ways than there are stars. You are the light of my world. Work hard, be disciplined, have fun, and go for your dreams. I believe in you – always.

To my mom, you have been there for me in ways I can't possibly imagine. You always believe in me. I love you. To my father, who taught me to love this country, this is for you. To my sisters, Jane and Martha, each of you have played a magnificent role in my life and helped to shape me into the person I am today. I couldn't ask for better sisters.

To all of my friends, who have shared my journey and offered their prayer and support along the way. I love you and count you as irreplaceable treasure. A special thank you to my good friend, Jason, you provided me steady footing to steer me through the tech world.

A special thank you to Laura, who provided invaluable assistance formatting and converting my book for electronic publishing. A special thank you to Rachel, who was the only author who would respond to my emails for advice. Thank you to one of my best friends in this world, Glenn, for helping me behind the scenes.

To God, who makes all things possible and calls things that are not as though they were. You are above description and alone are worthy. Thank you for Your presence, forgiveness and pursuing love.

Contents

Preface

*"Conservatives are responsible radicals.
During the American Revolution,
Conservatives would have been considered
liberal and today's Liberal would be the ruling
class oppressing the individual. The vast
majority of individuals are conservative with
their life, time, money and their family. How
then is it, that liberalism is the pervasive voice?
Who shapes this thinking? Individuals must
continually struggle through peaceful,
nonviolent means for the right to make their
decisions with minimal interference by those
who seek to rule. This political battle is life-
long and not a one-time event, which is why
conservatism remains revolutionary."*

Robert Lindsay, 2012

This book was written in an effort to offer a different perspective on areas of change needed in the United States. The bulk of this book was completed in December 2012. There has been a lot of editing the last six months, but the body of work detailed in my book, is a prelude to the current events/scandals happening in the news today. Rise Up is primarily about America expecting more from their elected leaders and evaluating their progress at the voter box. Americans own this country and while the federal government appears to be absent in leadership, the primary stock holders, Americans, do not appear to be anymore invested in the process. The preface is long, but worth the read. I love this country and if you are reading this book, my hope is that you will show your love by not standing idly by and watching what is happening, but be a voice – a non-violent, peaceful, voice that uplifts the Constitution and promote individual liberty and responsibility. That is the way to restore

America's economy and the spirit of the "American Dream."

 A reoccurring theme will be surrounding a resurgent economic recovery. Many people know there are more than two schools of thought on stimulating today's economy in America. Two of the most prevalent philosophies are Keynesian Economics and Supply-Side Economics. Keynesian Economics promotes a public sector influence on the economy that advocates putting checks and balances in place to insure that an even playing field towards financial prosperity exists and that oversight is provided through the federal government (Keynesian Economics, www.econlib.org). Supply-Side Economics encourages minimizing obstacles for people to produce goods and services, thus allowing individuals to reap the financial rewards associated with their hard work and personal initiative (Fax, 2011). Of course, these two examples are primitive in nature, but it gives the basic difference between the two philosophies. While Supply Side encourages less federal regulation and involvement, it recognizes the need for accountability and oversight. Even Adam Smith, who wrote "The Wealth of Nations" admitted government, has a role in economic growth as long as it does not disrupt the process (Smith, 1904).

I have no education or work history in politics or studying economic history, trends and growth. I am a therapist by trade. In fact, I work for a non-profit and work with low-income families who are usually on Medicaid. My paycheck ultimately comes from the tax payers. I am writing this book as an American who believes in the Constitution. Being conservative in the social work profession is challenging at times. Most in my field appear to be operating from a liberal philosophy. I often hear other therapists discouraged about their clients not trying harder in therapy to work on their issues. There are many parallels between the therapeutic process and the "Nanny State" mentality. A good therapist assist clients work towards self-determination and throughout the book there will be references to therapy to illustrate comparisons between the role of government and the role of the individual. The goal is to discuss possible solutions to broad topics most people view as important when discussing the future of our country.

My heart believes in this country. The United States of America is still the best country in the world. I was taught early on the joy of loving this country. Seeing the American people as the underdog; fighting and scraping our way against the most powerful ruler of the day in the British Empire. Our founders and the people who followed them looked into the eyes of tyranny and said, "We want liberty." Our founders rose up and dared to go to war against the greatest army in the world at that time and believed they could win. Our founders drafted a beautiful, timeless document that promotes the individual with creativity woven within the text that celebrates our Creator, embraces our talents and gifts and promotes a society where all are free to pursue life, liberty and happiness.

America has a long history of thinking about what is deemed impossible and making it possible. We are over-comers. We turn dreams into reality. America is the one who looks at the Moon at night and say, "Let's go there." And do it. It is in America where light can go from candle to electricity. America sets the standard for the world. We consider options and think within and out of the box. We are the type of republic that can embrace the possibility that while we have experts who believe they know what is best for our country and within the same breath, accept a layman coming along who may have a piece of the puzzle to add to the solution.

I believe politicians, lawyers, special interest groups and economic educators get fixated on their respected turfs and become entrenched, unable to move in a solution-focused manner. The inflexibility gives way to inactivity and inactivity results in stagnant deal making. The end result is poor outcomes for the people of this country. A large part of the reason deals are being made and nothing is getting done to move our country forward is the people in politics have made things way too complicated. Simple does not necessarily imply stupidity. Simple can be very, very smart. This book will attempt to make things simpler and allow the experts to complicate my efforts. I will present a new federal tax code, governmental agencies needing to restructure and those needing elimination, I will discuss the role of government in the United States, and a plan for the Republican Party to move the conservative agenda past those who already support them, but to carry that message to the masses.

The proposals set forth in this book are easy to read and follow. It is written by a layman and is intended to be uncomplicated. The experts can pick it apart and determine if there is any validity to it. I would be foolish to believe that I alone came up with the answers to solve our nation's issues when we have the greatest minds in the world actively seeking solutions and common ground. I am not that arrogant. I am simply optimistic and in love with this country. As I noted above, this country is so great, so free that maybe, just maybe, a layman can come up with possibilities that promote thought, dialogue and a coming together to get something done for the good of our country...for the good of the people. As Americans, we send representatives to govern for the good of the country which translates to the good of the people. We don't have time to go up to Washington, D.C. and take the reins of this country. We are busy making this country great by making dreams a reality. I am not calling for a people's rule or some type of populist movement. I am calling for our representatives to lead and for the people to remember that the representatives work for us, the people, and those representatives are to be evaluated on their performance. If they do well, they get rehired. If they don't perform then they get let go. It is that simple.

The recommended tax code is composed of four categories. The goal for the tax code is everyone pays into the system. Let me repeat that statement. Everyone pays into the federal tax system. Allow it to sink in for a minute. Everyone pays into the federal tax system. The rate is affordable for all identified tax payers. The big difference is there are zero deductions. Individuals can do without deductions and credits. Paying just the rate through their income each month eliminates filing at the end of the year. It also means America can make cuts that matter. This plan can make fundamental changes by drastically reducing the size of the government run agencies such as the Internal Revenue Service. Again, the rate is set up so that all that work pay into the system.

      This is important to note because currently there are about 47% of the American population not paying federal taxes (Sahadi, 2009). Each may contribute to pay roll taxes but not federal taxes. All, who live in this country, need to pay into the federal tax system. Raising taxes on the wealthy only goes so far. Some studies report allowing the Bush Tax Cuts to expire raises federal revenue by 100 billion annually (Bradford, 2012). When one looks at that amount compared to the national debt and our annual trillion dollar short fall then it is not that much. Increasing the size of the pie both with the economy and the tax base is the key. All people who live in this country need to pay into the federal tax system if we are going to pay taxes. It is not the responsibility of some to pay all the bills just because they have money. Adding tax money from 47% of those who currently don't pay into the system is the best way to increase tax revenue...and the fairest.

Many will implode over this seemingly dishonorable decision to eliminate credits and deductions, but think through the tax deduction system. It serves two possible street-wise rationales. Politicians can spin it however, but the gut of it is pretty simple. If an individual's tax rate is 25% and he or she only pays 15% then the individual perceives he or she is getting a deal. It is a lot like getting 10 percent off at a sale. People like deals. The other rationale is to condition behavior for the betterment of society. Think about it. A person gets a tax credit for adding energy efficient windows or having children or a tax rebate for purchasing a certain kind of car, charitable giving, etc. The conditioning is not bad in nature and encourages positive behaviors, but the real question is, do we want government to condition our behaviors? Where does it stop?

Consider New York City and the push there by the Mayor to make soft drinks more than 20oz illegal in restaurants (Francescani, 2012). Another example is the public school system evaluating our children lunches to determine if what is packed from home is healthy and what is not healthy (Boyle, 2012). There have been some embarrassing moments lately where the government has overstepped its role and is dictating to the people. It is the other way around. We own this country. We, the American people, employee elected officials. We fund the public school system. Government and the elected officials work for the American people, not the other way around.

The intent of the Mayor of New York may not be bad. We are an obese nation. Individuals need to address their health issues. Here is the question. Do you believe you are in a better position to take care of you or do you believe government is better at taking care of you? If it is the latter, in regards to your ability to make healthy decisions for yourself and family, then the underlying assumption from the government is, "We, the people, are too lazy and undisciplined to care for ourselves without the government doing it for us." This may be true for the individual, but it is the individual's right to choose to be lazy. It is the individual's right to eat how he or she wants. To say otherwise contradicts our Constitution and the initial rationale for seeking independence and fighting for individual freedom. We don't need deductions to shape behavior. Americans are the most generous people on the planet. We not only give more as individuals but as a nation. Let's not forget, when the government gives aid to another country that money came from the people. Government does not produce anything without the people. We are its life and we are its master, not the other way around.

There are many in this country in favor of a Fair Tax System being implemented as a national sales tax (Worstall, 2012) or just an across the board flat tax . Personally, I would have no problem with this system with a flat or fair tax. If it was completely up to me I would institute the following: 12% income tax for all who work. 12% capital gains tax. 06% corporate tax on all businesses. 03% national sales tax on all good sold in the United States. No loop holes. No deductions. No way for anyone to get out of any of it. The federal government would have what it has coming in and would be forced to operate its budget on that amount.

However, for the last 100 years, we have had a progressive tax and no one seems to have the nerve to push for a flat tax. Politicians can't get behind the Fair or Flat tax process because we have always been a progressive tax nation. Our culture is if you have more you pay more. Politicians won't vote for it out of fear, but not because it is a bad idea. The goal of taxation, in my opinion, is for it to decrease over time, not increase or go back and forth. However, rather

than throwing the whole concept out the
window, I recommend a 03% national sales tax
with a law passed stipulating the tax can never
exceed 07% and can only increase to 07% if
income taxes decrease proportionately.
Instituting a national sales tax of this rate, while
restricting government's so-called right to
increase it at their leisure, may result in
approximately 300 billion or more in revenue.
It also serves as a method for all to pay into the
federal tax system. This involves those living in
America who are not working or who are here
illegally and not paying into the federal tax
system through the income tax system.

The capital gains tax is divided up in
three tiers based on income. I don't like it
because it punishes success, but if I can get the
other elements of this book put into practice
then the wealthy will not have a problem paying
more in capital gains. Those who oppose the
current rate do so because they want the rich to
start businesses and not just live off

investments. The opposition would argue the millionaire is not actively creating jobs through actual job creation by starting a business from the ground up it is fair to tax them more. This does not mean they are not building businesses. Through their investments they are allowing companies to grow, prosper and thereby adding employees as they go. Plus, it's their money to do as they wish.

My rationale for keeping the rate is that it has shown it works. Under George W Bush when he and Congress agreed to lower the capital gains rate from 20% to 15% in 2003 the federal government increased federal revenue more (2003 – 2007) than at any other time in our history (Dwyer, 2010). History shows when the rate is low the economy thrives. In reviewing President Clinton's economy growth please remember that he reduced the capital gains tax in 1997 to 20% which accounts for a lot of the growth taking place during his next four years in office (Foster, 2008). Individuals risk financial loss to invest in the Stock Market. If you make the risk too great for someone to invest they won't. They will sit on their money and wait things out. That approach creates stagnation which is the opposite of growth.

The corporate tax code is reduced, making it one of the lowest rates in the world. The federal government receives minimal revenue from the corporate tax rate (about 9% of its total budget), but the way it is reported the individual could easily think the margin is larger and more significant (Williams, 2011). Dropping the rate to the one recommended also takes into account the national sales tax. With that included, it is still one of the lowest rates in the world. Increasing job growth and reducing the unemployment rate is accomplished in the private sector. Small business growth produces the majority of jobs in this country. Reducing their financial burden allows more profit. More profit promotes opportunity for expansion.

Expansion means hiring. Growth and more employees mean more federal revenue.

The national debt is America's greatest enemy. While terrorism and the rise of Islamic Radicals is certainly a national security concern, the greatest enemy to America is us. Being in debt to other countries and needing foreign oil places America in a position to compromise our values and the core beliefs that make us the greatest country in the world. Paying down our national debt and balancing our annual budget should be the primary objective of any administration regardless of party. In my proposed plan, the intake from taxation accounts for 4 trillion annually. The annual budget on expenses is to be 2.7 trillion or less annually. The goal is to pay 500 billion or more towards the principal of the national debt and getting the debt level to 35% or less of Gross Domestic Product (GDP) by 2048. This needs to be the priority. In hindsight, Republicans in power in 2004 should have made paying down the national debt from 4.5 trillion to 1 trillion in 2008. Consider the position the United States would have for its citizens and the world at large during the economic crash. Think of the value of the dollar.

My point is simple. Debt is not good for the individual, family, business or for a government. Debt may help for a short period, but never to be dependent on. That in itself creates dependency. It splits allegiances and creates compromises that divide versus unites. Is it any wonder we are split as a nation? Is it any reason we are left impotent to effect change in places in the world where we once commanded respect. Paying down the debt, living within our means and balancing the budget is key to our nation thriving in a world that outwardly wants to see us fail.

Entitlements are confused with social programming and this needs to be clarified to the public. Social programming needs to be time-limited with emphasis placed on reclaiming individual responsibility. The 1996 Welfare Reform Act promoted this concept and has been successful (Archer, 1998). Strong changes need to occur within Unemployment Benefits, Food Stamps, Medicaid and other related assistance programs. These program need to promote short-term help and not dependency.

Medicare and Social Security are an Entitlement and needs to be considered an honoring program. This will rub conservatives the wrong way. These two programs involved individuals paying into each to get a payout down the road. The overwhelming majority of seniors in our society have worked hard all their lives and contributed to all aspects of our economy. Honoring each of them by providing through taxation a program that assists them in medical coverage is an American value. These programs need to be made financially solvent by increasing the age requirements for individuals younger than 45 years of age and be able to stand on its own by being properly managed, but is a program worth having to demonstrate the respect and appreciation to those who have paved the way.

Let me emphasize. No true conservative or anyone else wants those who have real needs; whether it be Down syndrome, Autism, or other impairments minimizing their ability to care for him or herself to be left without assistance. No one wants seniors (despite popular beliefs, conservatives do have mothers and fathers) to be cut off and receive no assistance or services (Wehner, 2011). The goal is to differentiate from senior programming and those on social programs. In safety net programming (social programming), screen out those who can return to the work force from those who cannot care for themselves. Create standards and policies that promote individual rights to self-determination and eliminate codependency.

Chapter 1
New World Order:
11-7-12

"However [political parties] may now and then answer popular ends, they are likely in the course of time and things, to become potent engines, by which cunning, ambitious, and unprincipled men will be enabled to subvert the power of the people and to usurp for themselves the reins of government, destroying afterwards the very engines which have lifted them to unjust dominion."

George Washington, Farewell Address, 1776

America's Liberalism

We will never know if Governor Romney would have made a great president. We will never know if having a business man in the White House would have made a difference for our country and for future generations. There is a new world order on the rise in America. It is called liberalism. The Left attacked the Governor relentlessly and in the end, the American people spoke through reelecting President Obama. Now, the pressure is on the President to showcase to the world that his brand of liberalism is the future. While I hope any President is successful in leading our country, I don't desire for the United States of America to become a European-style society. America is unique, or at least, *was* unique. The economy, the direction of the country is now Obama's to own. Whatever happens on his watch at this point is truly his to own. Though he still may blame Bush or the Republicans, he is the leader and the results rest on him.

Success or failure, it is all him. So how can Republicans help our leader?

Republicans need to show resolve and allow the Bush Tax Cuts to expire (This book was completed in December 2012 and I decided to leave it as written). Both President Obama and President Clinton were so adamant during the presidential campaign that the Clinton years produced so many jobs and the economy thrived at that level of taxation. The Republicans need to hold the line on fiscal responsibility and tie it to: *Cut, Cap, Reform and Balance*. This is an opportunity to witness one of two things over the next four years. Either President Obama is right and his way is the way to follow for America or he is wrong and the economy continues to tank. Either way, the evidence is in allowing his policies to work and take effect.

This is an opportunity for the Republicans to emerge and stand up. Republicans will be blamed no matter what happens for any and all the bad that happens. The media and Democrats will not allow Republicans to appear victorious. Republicans need to instead focus on being the stable, well-intentioned adult in a bad divorce situation. The Democrats represent the adult who capitulates and allows those they think they control to do what they want in an effort to win them over. The mistake on both parties is viewing the people as children. While America has some adult children out there who won't take responsibility for their lives and want freedom to be devoid of any moral reasoning, the majority will be embarrassed by our government's antics and will yearn for real leaders to emerge.

In truth, there is a significant amount of the population in America living off governmental assistance. How can a person or a people be objective about the overall good of the country when there is such a high percentage benefiting from the very policies sinking our currency? They can't. America is torn on the direction of their country. On one hand, you can say the people sent a message by reelecting President Obama. On the other hand, the people reelected the Republicans as the majority in the House which holds the purse strings. Again, we are divided and Republicans need to fulfill their pledge, their mandate by the people, to hold Washington, D.C. accountable and get our fiscal house in order. Republicans need to take a page out of the Democrat, community organizer play-book and use crisis, like the fiscal cliff, to promote conservatism. The message is simple: *Cut, Cap, Reform and Balance.* Everything Republicans do, propose, say, release to the press needs to be those four words.

The Elephant in the Room

In therapy, there is a therapeutic strategy to expose the "elephant" in the room. In some cases, therapists may add color to it by calling it a pink elephant. When you meet with a family, they are so close to the issues a lot of time they cannot see the issues staring them in the face. We refer to that in some ways as becoming aware of this huge potential problem in the room that everyone steps around and refuses to acknowledge. Even though it makes everyone adjust their ability to maneuver within the family; the family has grown used to it and accepted it as being normal. When a good therapist starts working with a family and begins to connect the puzzle together and help the family see things more objectively, it is amazing how nauseated a family can become when they clearly see what they have been putting up with and labeling as "normal." Once the individuals in the family, and the family as a whole, embrace their brokenness and embrace the real obstacles in their lives, then, and only then, can real change-talk begin and a real plan towards growth occurs.

The "pink elephant" in the room in Washington is the two parties can't work together. The ideology of conservatism and liberalism are incompatible. There is no compromise between Republicans and Democrats. Any compromise is really concession from the other. Republicans want to bring spending under control, reform social programs, entitlements and deal with the debt. Democrats want to increase revenue to the government, keep social programs and entitlements the way they are and want a bigger federal government. There is no victory to be had here in fighting against the Democrat machine and those who elected them back to power. In the same way, Democrats can't expect to compromise with a conservative Republican. The two ideologies, if each is true to their stance on government, have entirely two different philosophies with almost no common ground.

Put it this way. Consider you have a 25 or 45 year old son. He doesn't have a job and expects his parents to foot the bill for all he does. His father still does his laundry and makes him breakfast in the morning and does not expect any effort on his son's part to care for his self or to contribute to his care. The mother disagrees with the approach of the father and wants her son to get a job, take responsibility and move out in 6 months because she believes this is best for the son and for the good of the family. At some point, if the parents don't find common ground, they will split; each scratching their head over the positions the other took in regards to what was best for their son and the family. Each parent blames the other and each has valid points in his or her own mind on why the other is wrong.

The son is in the normal range of functioning and could be independent if he chose to be. From his perspective, he has no reason to change. He has it made. He has a roof over his head, food on the table, most likely cable television, and the ability to come and go. Attempts by his parents to get him to do anything are met with outbursts, protest and reasons why things need to stay the same. One parent wants to take a stand and the other wants to enable the son to avoid conflict and to satisfy something within his own need as a parent. The son is not entirely to blame here. The parents are responsible for not only raising this son to have such entitled expectations, but reinforcing these expectations at his current age. What motivation does he have to change? His behavior serves his own needs, but also, his behavior is fulfilling some need in his parents too or they would not keep reinforcing it. One parent couldn't take it anymore and one decided to put up with it.

This is an example of America. This is an example of liberalism. In order for the Republicans to expose the lie of liberalism they must not give in and compromise. Doing nothing is better than living in collusion with the Democrats. They must stand together and provide a clear contrast for America to see.

Republicans must develop a strategy promoting conservatism and deliver that message to the American people through a strategic marketing campaign process. When the pain of staying the same exceeds the pain of staying of change the American people will cry out for real change. That is what America is doing now except they have been sold a bill of goods that in the end will taste like sand and not the sparkling water they were so richly promised. The real lie of liberalism is that real success is a right and not the result of work. Whether you are speaking of character, building a business, building a family or being discipline with your own finances? All successful endeavors require focus, patience and dedication. There is nothing easy about success. Liberalism says we can have the goodies without putting in the time, the sweat equity required to achieve. This is not true.

These are critical times in America. Other times presented their own challenges, but as we have increased our command and dependency on technology, information is available to the people like never before. There is no room for politicians who won't get the job done. Since America is not satisfied that President Obama had enough time to get his job done and allowed him another four years, I think it important to provide a clear contrast for Americans on his vision for America and the Republicans' vision for America. Republicans have an enormous amount of influence and authority. Republicans maintain control of the money and do not need to be bullied into compromising just because someone has to cry uncle.

Cut, Cap, Reform & Balance

In family therapy, a good therapist teaches parents to identify appropriate expectations for their children and hold to their principles. The mistake parents often make is giving ground to their children and then trying to take it back. I was speaking with a mother and she has her four year old set up with a flat screen, cable and a computer in his room already to "help him sleep through the night." I don't see that turning out well. Republicans need to hold their position and every negotiation needs to be about: *Cut, Cap, Reform and Balance*. *Cut* federal spending and not just lower projected growth of spending. *Cap* the amount the federal government can spend annually. *Reform* federal agencies, programs, taxes, etc to reflect the desired fiscal responsibilities we want our government to represent. *Balance* the damn budget.

The Democrats embrace liberalism and they won't compromise their values. Why should Republicans? Any discussion that does not include *Cut, Cap, Reform and Balance* needs to halt immediately. It surprises me how directionless the Republicans seem to be at times. They just need to stick with the four pillars mentioned above for now and work towards tax reform. It is no more complicated than that. They have the House, which means they control the money. They are in a good position to dictate play, but when I watch the Republicans as an outsider, they appear to act like out of town guests who do not know where the bath room is while visiting the host's home. It does not inspire nor does it command respect.

America has to bottom out for real change to happen. Republicans cannot be afraid for this to happen. America may have to rebuild. As a therapist, I have met with many parents who are being held hostage by their kids. The parents are afraid. If the parent takes a certain action with their child the parent worries how the child will respond, rather than what is best for the child, the family and the overall situation. If the parent doesn't do anything then the parent feels stuck. Once parents get in this boat of constantly second-guessing their decision making and how the child will respond, it is extremely hard to stop rowing the boat and change directions. It exemplifies where Republicans are in our culture today. Hitting bottom is bad, but real change usually emerges from bad stuff happening. Lasting change for America is not easy and comes down to which ideology does America want?

Republicans have to hold the line fiscally without flinching or being afraid of the next election. Those scared of losing their seats need to leave anyway. America needs strong leadership. America needs the Republicans to hold the line and establish solid boundaries and expectations. The Republicans need to continually link every deal or comment back to *Cut, Cap, Reform* and *Balance* (I have said this already, right).   No matter which avenue the Republicans take they will be blamed for any negative results (I have said this too). If they stand against the rule of the Democrats and hold the line they will be blamed for a stagnant economy and for being racist towards the first black president. If they try to be moderate and give in on certain things, but hold the line in other places then the Republicans will be blamed for what does not work. If they completely step aside and allow the President to implement policies and run the country as he sees fit, the Republicans will still be blamed if progress is not noted over the next four years. The Republicans cannot win no matter which way they lead.

While the American people are smart, there is a high percent that get "stuff" from the government and like the adult child mentioned above they don't want to see that changed. The Republicans need to command the media by taking a page out of the Democrat play book and keep America up to speed with what the Republicans are doing, why they are doing it and allow the President to take full credit for what happens the next four years. Two things may happen. Either liberalism is exposed and the people see it or the president is successful and the country is better off. We shall see what the two parties do, but conservatism works. If it is to come back, the people must want it or it has no chance.

Conservative Principles are Timeless

Conservatism represents best what this country has and is about. Individual liberties and the ability to start from nothing and achieve great things is what many refer to as the "American Dream." We are the greatest country in the world. We believe this, not because we are arrogant or conceited, but quite the opposite. We believe and live this out before the world to provide hope that people can govern themselves and, in so doing, provide a Land marked with more opportunity for its people. Liberalism is a broken promise. It can never be sustained. Margret Thatcher, the great leader of Great Britain in the 1980s, famously proclaimed, "The problem with socialism is eventually you run out of other people's money" (Thatcher, 2011). It ends in not fulfilling the desired upon goal because it fosters dependency rather than self-sufficiency. Liberalism devalues the individual by artificially coddling the individual. In therapy, we refer to this process as codependency. It means what it sounds like. People become dependent on something else that interferes with them moving forward in life and achieving their own goals.

Prior to having children, my wife, Julie and I had just the two of us around the house. We both had advanced degrees and bright futures. We both served humanity through government supported services. She was in education. I was a social worker. We had accumulated some debt and made some poor financial decisions along the way. We figured it would work out over time. We did not put extra energy into paying things off. Instead, we kicked the financial can down the road.

When Julie became pregnant with our first child, it was a blessing and a surprise to us. We knew we could not continue to accumulate debt and with Julie wanting to go to part-time status, I had to pick up another job. I have worked seven days a week from 2007 through 2012 in an attempt to pay off debt and off-set what we lost when Julie gave up some of her time in the work force. It wasn't until we were forced to do something about our finances that we actually stepped up and took the initiative. Liberalism props people up artificially. Liberalism conveys to the individual he or she does not need to struggle, but he or she is to be cared for and provided without the individual having real skin in the game. It is unhealthy. Individuals, when compelled too, rise up to meet challenges and are resilient by nature. Expecting people to be responsible for their own life is nothing short of the very living definition of freedom.

We have all heard the term "Tough Love." It is often misquoted or misunderstood. The explanation of tough love is simple. Set limits, be firm, yet fair in decision making, and allow the individual to be responsible for him or herself (Wardrop, 2009). To continue propping someone up or bailing the person out of trouble only reinforces to the individual that he or she is somehow insulated from the realities of the world. I see this all the time with parents who continue to make excuses for their children's behaviors or decision making. They want to do the right thing by protecting him or her, but the enemy of the best is often the good. Sometimes people have to fail. Sometimes people have to hit the rocks at the bottom of the imaginary cliff of life because they did something stupid or without much thought. Sometimes bad stuff happens with the person not necessarily doing anything wrong. Life happens.

As people, we have to learn the art and skill of persevering. We live in a much insulated world today. We don't have to gut through things like people years ago. This is both good and bad. The good is obvious. Advances in technology have made life easier in many ways and has expanded our knowledge in the area of discovery. This is good. The bad often goes without much notice. The bad shows itself in the number of divorces in our country. Fifty percent of first marriages, sixty-seventy percent of second marriages and seventy-four percent of third marriages end in divorce in the United States (Banschick, 2012).   If you don't like your marriage, divorce and move on. If you don't like your supervisor, get another job. If you don't like this or that, then trade it out and get something else. As people, we don't have to work through issues or circumstances with the same level of determination as our founders, great grandparents or grandparents. We have, in some ways, become servants to the Technology Age.   We have the ability to cocoon ourselves in our homes and not leave. We can interact with others through social media, order food and grocery shop on-line as well as buy anything else we need off the internet. We can feel protected as we isolate ourselves from others. If we have kids, we can put them in front of the television or purchase a DVD and allow others to entertain them to avoid interaction, avoid conflict, and ultimately, avoid growth and intimacy. It is through struggle, through conflict, through the art of persevering that real growth happens. The old work-out adage, "No Pain...No Gain" fits well here. I am sure there is some loon who will inform me the adage mentioned above is actually out of date because pain is an indicator the muscle is being overworked and needs rest and to continue to push through the exercise when the body has warned you of its limit will result in injury. You are probably right, but you are also a bore and missed the whole point.

Working through issues and learning how to work with others is a lost art. We text; e-mail is so "Old School." Society is dealing with social media bullying. Kids get hammered on line by the latest gossip by their peers (Kang, 2011) and parents are oblivious because there is no true interaction and communication going on in the family. Businesses fax, text and do so many things electronically that again, the art of cultivating relationships is not as present. We have seen this clearly the last four years with our politicians who cannot for their life get out of the way of their own egos and show America and the world they can work together. Leadership at home, in business and in politics is about working together, cultivating relationships and learning how to communicate with one another in such a way that all are empowered to achieve great things.

Conservatism promotes the individual and self-responsibility. Conservatism promotes liberty and the individual rights of others. A politician, a business person, an individual who follows conservative ideas wins. My book embraces a conservative philosophy that calls for less federal oversight on the individual. It is a plan that has the opportunity to be embraced by a majority if seen in the correct light. In our current world it is too easy to view politics by party. There is much in this book that conservatives may disagree with and not embrace. My goal is to promote a strategy to improve economic growth while also exposing America's identity issue raging across our Land like a California wild life fire burning out of control.

Chapter 2: Taxes Made Simple

"I have one other request. As representatives of Main Street America, would you please send Washington a message: `Get your hands out of our pockets, get control of your own budget, and let us get on with the job of rebuilding America.' Tax rates are prices -- prices for working, saving, and investing. And when you raise the price of those productive activities, you get less of them and more activity in the underground economy --tax shelters and leisure pursuits. You in small business understand that you can't force people to buy merchandise that isn't selling by raising your price. But too many in Washington and across the country still believe that we can raise more revenues from the economy by making it more expensive to work, save, and invest in the economy."

Ronald Reagan, 1983

Tax Plan

I am not wealthy. I would love to be one day as a result of my work, but it is not my goal and it is not the norm within my profession. My goal is to help others. As a therapist, I want to provide quality treatment to individuals and families, so each can gain insight into their issues and overcome these issues to achieve their desired goals. As a supervisor, who oversees employees in a small, non-profit agency, I want each employee to learn the value of developing self-awareness and practicing, with integrity, that which they are paid to teach the kids and families we are called to help.

I lead with this introduction to a revised tax plan because most seemingly have an angle when they propose tax reform. While I may have an angle, I am not sure I know what it is at this time. In my heart, my angle is what is the best way to stimulate the economy, grow jobs, and in the process, create the revenue needed by the federal government? Why does the federal government need revenue? We have debt to pay, a country to defend, and a country to run. We need revenue until we truly decide what role government is to play with social programming. National defense, social programs, entitlements make up the biggest expense of what the federal government pays out. While we have to cut expenses, politicians will haggle over what to cut until the people of this country make it clear what the role of government is to be for the individual.

Everyone knows there the federal government spends a lot of money. I am not sure everyone agrees spending is a serious issue and needs to be dealt with directly and responsibly. While the founders would roll over in their graves at the level of taxation in any current political party plan, it is the world in which we live at present time. Politicians working together for the people are expected, right? Not happening, is it? The tax plan reflects that the federal government needs 30%

or less of an individual's income. The *ideal* goal of total taxation on the individual from the federal government needs to be no more than 15% of an individual's income. We aren't there yet, due to so much division, so 30% needs to be the maximum taxation until things change. There will be those sighting this one statement as being proof that higher taxation raises revenue and justifies why tax hikes work. Wrong. My goal is to continue reducing taxes over time until America gets to what it has to have monetarily and nothing more. The goal of taxation is to go down, not up. Individuals need to keep their money – not government. A sign of a vibrant economy is one where taxes descend rather than ascend. We aren't there yet, but we could be and for that to happen the people have to rise up.

There is an old story about a mother cooking a pot roast with her fourteen year old daughter. The daughter has helped her mother for years preparing this meal. The daughter notices her mother cutting off the end of the roast before putting it in the pan. The daughter knows her mom's answer before she asks it, but decides to ask again. "Mom," the daughter asks, "why do you cut the end of the roast off like that when you have room in the pan." The mother responds, "this is the way my mother taught me when I was a child." The daughter accepts the response, but files it away to ask her grandmother the next time she sees her. The next month, the daughter travels with her mother to see her grandmother. During the course of the visit, the fourteen year old daughter brings up the preparation for the roast with her grandmother and mother. The grandmother, now in her eighties, smiles as her granddaughter ask her about cutting off the end of the roast as she prepared it with the daughter's mother all those years ago. The grandmother looks at her child, who is now fifty years old and the beautiful jewel of a granddaughter, who is so inquisitive. She responds simply with the slightest of giggle. "Child, the reason I cut the end of the roast off years ago had to do with our pan being too small and I couldn't get the whole roast in it."

This represents taxation. It actually represents a great many things. Just because we have done it the same way doesn't mean it is the way to do it. This is true individually, collectively, in business and as a country. Thinking outside of the box and asking questions is important. Accepting the status quo is not American. Americans don't accept something just because someone said it. Americans ask why. Americans look for better ways to accomplish the objective. Americans strive to be the best, to be number one.

Fifteen percent needs to be the future max on any individual income tax. Ideally a flat tax would be preferred, but even with a progressive tax it needs to max out at fifteen percent. Any more than 15% is wasteful spending on the part of the federal government and dishonoring to the individual who worked to earn it. Self-Employed individuals have to pay the full 15% in pay roll tax as I mentioned earlier. This is a heavy burden on small businesses. One day the pay roll tax needs to fade away, especially when it comes to the employer matching the employee's tax for Social Security and Medicare. Again, taxation needs to decrease over time, not increase. A tax system decreasing on its citizens confirms a healthy, robust economy. The bigger the pie of revenue means the more people are paying into the tax system which means more businesses and more jobs.

Again, we are discussing federal income taxes. An individual still has to pay state and local taxes on top of everything else. Individuals across the country need to ask "how much of my hard earned money am I allowed to keep?" That sentence alone needs to send shivers down everyone's spine, for it is your money first and not the government. States taxing income will increase total taxation. I live in North Carolina and the Income Tax Rate is around seven percent. People in California, who love taxes, pay approximately 13% in state income. This is on top of federal and local taxes. People in Texas and Florida have no state income tax. High taxing states tend to be liberal in their voting history, so they can remain the beacon of light for the liberal agenda.

Why won't raising taxes on the rich work to stimulate the economy? Here are my thoughts on the subject. The wealthy (not to be confused with small business owners) will make their money. Small business owners, who are willing to risk their capital to start a business, will make their money too. In other words, the five percent (errs) will be just fine. If taxes are raised on them, they will adjust. For example, a business owner, who generates two million in sales and employees four people, will calculate what he or she needs to make once the increased tax system goes into place. If he or she put $300,000 in their pocket last year, he or she will again this year. If that means he or she needs to cut positions and go down to fewer employees to cover the increased taxation or charge more to the consumer then that is the cost of business.

However, if the government makes the taxes work for businesses then the business owner has more capital. Having more capital may mean that the owner does not cut anyone and instead risks more capital which results in hiring more people. The increase in expansion plus the addition of new employees increases the amount of revenue contributed to the federal government. It really is that simple. The rich will stay rich regardless and making them pay more only hurts those working for the business owner. It also hurts the lawn maintenance entrepreneur, the self-employed house keeper and the countless jobs out there depending on people to have a little extra money to indulge in luxury-related services.

Everyone ends up getting hurt by taking more money away from those who have it. Contrary to popular belief, no one works for a company or individual who doesn't have money. We need people to have money. We need the rich to be rich so we might have a shot at being rich too. Spreading wealth around and evening the playing field is fantasy. Life is not fair. Working hard, dreaming big and taking risks to achieve those dreams **IS** the "American Dream."

Federal spending needs to be 20% or lower than gross domestic product (GDP), and borrowing needs to be 35% or less than GDP. The below proposal is one that reflects the need to stimulate the economy, make needed "cuts" to federal spending and attempt to preserve the values that make the United States of America the greatest country in the world. The tax reform section offers the following:

- Closes the loop-holes that are often used to escape the responsibility of paying into the tax system. The tax is fixed. It is what a person or business pays. No tax credits, exemptions, deductions.

- Provides fair opportunity for all living in the United States of America to pay into the federal tax system.
- Provides the opportunity for all working people to pay into the tax system.
- Hold accountable those countries who are taxing our products in their respected countries.
- Rates are low enough that individual(s) and families can keep more of their money
- People do one of 3 things with money: 1) spend 2) give 3) save. No one buries money in the ground and does nothing with it. The more a person has, the more that person will spend, give and/or save – this is what grows the economy...this is what generates more revenue for the government

New Federal Government Tax Code:
Provides government what it needs to operate
on a 2.7 trillion budget. If it can operate on less
than 2.7, cuts are made and the remainder is
put into an account for states who need it for
natural disasters or if nation needs to go to war.
The amount over 2.7 goes to paying off the
national debt with the goal of paying it off by
2048 (if not before). There is no reason not to
pay at least 500 billion per year towards the
principle of the national debt.

New Tax Code:

Corporate Tax Rate: 06% (No deductions.
It is only for companies manufacturing or
producing goods in the United States.
Remember, businesses also pay 7.5% of pay roll
tax and will also pay the 3% national sales tax
recommended in this plan. If a person is self-
employed he or she pays the whole 15% of pay
roll tax. The business owner gets hit with the

corporate tax, pay roll tax and individual income tax at the federal level. Include liability coverage, miscellaneous fees, state, county and local taxes and businesses pay more than their fair share).

20%: (No deductions. For US-based companies manufacturing products overseas but counting themselves as a US company).

Capital Gains Tax: 15% ($700,000 to $9,000,000) / **25%** ($9,000,001 and up). Remember, this income was previously taxed under income when it was first earned. The earnings off the investment portion are considered "new" income from the federal government perspective. While Conservatives may insist I am a traitor for recommending a 25% rate for those making over 9 million on their investments, I can assure you that those in this bracket will be glad to pay this rate if the other recommendations in this book are approved.

Income Tax: 12% ($394,000 and up). **08%** (**$126,000 to $393,999). **05% (**$40,000 to $125,999). **01% (**$1,000 to $39,999). There will be no deductions of any kind. There would be no need to file at the end of the year. There are no protected tax shelters of any kind. All pay taxes on goods & income. Eliminate all loop holes that allow individuals to move money from one area to another to avoid paying taxes.

National Sales Tax: 03% (All people who buy things in the USA pay taxes. This solves issue of illegal(s) not paying into system. This provides across the board accountability and responsibility for all to pay into the system while reaping the benefit of living in this great nation. There needs to be clear limitations on government control over adjusting the percentage. For example, the tax can never exceed 7%. The goal is for taxes to always go down not up. If the national sales tax is a bust and no one votes for it then add 3% to each proposed tax rates already mentioned. Again, the goal is for all to pay into the system and like it or not there are people here illegally who don't pay taxes and need too. This goes for internet sales for federal taxes, not state taxes. I told you conservatives may have an issue with some of the ideas in this book).

Pay Roll Tax: 15.0% = 07.5% Employer + 07.5%Employee. Identify a time frame or method to eliminate employer contribution to this tax over time once entitlements can be reformed.

Value-Added Tax: There are countries who tax our products when our products arrive in their port. It is called a value-added tax (VAT). Our government also taxes American made products prior to leaving port for other countries. This tax on our part needs to be eliminated. Companies are getting double taxed. The United States needs to explore a VAT to imports from countries applying a VAT to our product(s). Free-Trade is ideal, but when America does not get the same treatment we need to go with Fair-Trade policies. 25% VAT on foreign goods may encourage Free-Trade.

As I have stated, the need for a simplified tax code is an absolute must to move our economy and country forward in the 21st century. The current code is so complicated that the Internal Revenue Service (IRS) has difficulty understanding the process. There is also the power and authority of the IRS that needs to be reduced. Regardless of political appointees and or independence from political oversight, an entity garnishing that much power is a recipe for disaster for the individual. Also, there is the status of fairness which is a huge topic on both sides of the political aisle. All need to pay taxes and all need to pay as he or she goes, so there is no end of the year submission or last minute finagling out of what is due. It doesn't get fairer than the code I recommend above. Will it strain the poor? Sure. The goal of poverty is not to make individuals comfortable in it, but to create motivation for each to rise up out of it. The middle class is where a society wants their poor to rise too with a possible hunger to go further. America represents opportunity, not complacency. The poor have to want to strive for more than staying poor and policies that placate them only dishonor their character to better themselves.

Inheritance, Gift, Estate & Miscellaneous Taxes

We need to eliminate the inheritance, gift and estate tax for individuals regardless of income status. Imagine having an extra $100,000. You cashed in on some investments, paid taxes on the extra income like a good citizen and know what you want to do with the earned money. You want to give it to your daughter as a gift. However, you can only give her $13,000 without it being taxed again. This is ridiculous and in my book, stealing. The government has no right to it. They would say, but is new income to the daughter and therefore needs to be taxed since it is her new money. What kind of corrupt, loan-shark-minded system do we just roll over and accept in this country? This money was taxed initially on the first time earned. It was taxed again through capital gains on what was deemed "new" on top of the initial investment. Now it is taxed again since it is "new" money to the daughter. The premise is the daughter did nothing to earn it, so therefore she needs to pay taxes on it. The underlying assumption by the government is the money ultimately belongs to the government and not the individual.

The inheritance and estate tax work the same way. The difference is it works on mainly wealthy people. The middle class and poor are taught through the media and other representatives to look the other way because it doesn't concern us. The government engages in bullying behavior when it colludes with us in this way. Everyone in the school system and those working with kids know the way you change bullying behavior is to change those who stand idly by and do nothing. Efforts to change the bully are ineffective and efforts to help the one being bullied are not always productive. It is the 90% who aren't impacted directly, but choose to look the other way, that is the key to change. It is the same here.

If I had a 100 million and I wanted to leave it to my kids, but died prior to being able to safeguard it through trusts and all types of legal protective jargon, then a huge percentage goes to government (Miller, 2012). When Clinton was president this tax was around 50%. It is ludicrous and should be considered thievery for the government to think they have a claim on another person's wealth and property after it has already been taxed.

Consider the gasoline tax. For those working or having enough income to purchase a vehicle we are taxed by our federal government and state for putting gasoline in our tanks. I understand the rationale for the gas tax. If you use the roads then you pay the tax. That seems to validate the Fair Tax concept. Individuals, paying for what he or she use is the concept for the Fair Tax. In my plan the federal gasoline tax would drop to 3% (national sales tax) from the 17+% it is now. This will help people at the pump by putting more money in the pocket of the individual.

Social Security income is yet another example of loan shark ethics by the federal government. The feds control the individual in requiring withdraw on each pay check. The automatic withdraw goes into an account the individual cannot access. The individual receives a lousy return on interest for the amount of years the money is invested. The individual cannot bequeath their investment to anyone and is forced to deal with restriction on the investment while being forced to participate in the social security program by the federal government.

Now, once the money is finally drawn upon by the individual in their sixties or so the money is taxed. Forget that the government has been using this money all along at no reimbursement to the individual for all these years. This is robbery and detrimental to our seniors. Social Security Income needs to be tax-free. There doesn't need to be a tax on this money. The government was able draw interest on all that was put into this fund for years upon years. There is no way the individual is receiving back their investment at the appropriate interest level paid out. That amount goes to the government and if the government claims they didn't get a percentage of the interest then that further illustrates why they don't need to be in control of it.

There are federal taxes upon taxes I am not familiar with that are so woven into our society that I can't begin to examine all of them. They just need to be eliminated. Not reduced or restructured but eliminated. Taxing the snot out of people and businesses is just rude and unappreciative for what the individual or business has done to help add to the economy. Remember, the government works for the people. The government belongs to the people, not the other way around. If all are paying into the tax structure as I propose then we will have more than enough revenue to continue providing the things we, the people, want the government to provide. We don't need to be excessively taxed whether we are directly impacted or not. It is too easy to say the rich can pay more because they have money while the middle class is sucking wind and the poor stand idly by. This is wrong for anyone and the 90% need to stand up and say, "Cut it out. We don't treat people this way." All people need to keep as much of their money as possible and all need to pay taxes.

If the national sales tax is not an option because it requires too much to do to get passed into legislation then the income tax rate needs to go up by 3% in each of the four proposed federal income tax categories. Instituting a national sales tax is the fairest way to insure all pay federal taxes. It makes the most sense if it is capped so politicians cannot jack it up on a whim. Remember, the Supreme Court struck down taxing income in the 1800s because it was not constitutional (Wunder, 2010). The progressives amended the Constitution in the early 1900s so they could tax income and law-makers have been tax-crazed ever since. Again, if we are to have taxes on income then everyone paying taxes is fair and makes the most sense.

I know that when the poor are hit with a tax on their income somebody's brain is going to explode. They will say this is unfair, it is regressive and that there is no way this is to be allowed. This is non-sense. Will it increase their financial burden? Yes. Is it the right thing to do? Yes. All need to pay taxes. There is no excuse for people being exempt. If we are going to have a tax system in this country then the fair and responsible thing is for all to pay into it. It would be like living in a family where only certain members in the family did chores and the others did nothing, but the ones who did nothing actually enjoyed the fruits of all the labors. All need to be involved in the process and responsible for the upkeep of this country. This is very important in dealing with spending. *The goal is for the poor to move to the middle class and the middle class to move up to the next tier financially. We want a conveyer belt system where people grow their income and are self-determined. We want people to dream and achieve.*

Enabling people to stay the same and shun responsibility goes against every position I ever had as a therapist. You want people to identify their goals and strive to achieve. You want them to deal with the obstacles in their lives and learn positive ways to work through difficulties. You want them to be optimistic about their future and to take charge of their life. Overcoming and persevering is a large part of life. Once I determine an individual does not want to work in therapy and likes the dysfunction the way it is and only wants to come and talk with me, then we begin working towards termination of therapy. Maybe other therapists would be glad to take the person's money to talk, but that is not my style. I am glad to help and to help others achieve their stated goals and ambitions, but I am not content to prop individuals up and pretend they are doing the right thing by giving up on their hopes of overcoming the obstacles in their life. These concepts in therapy are exactly what are needed in regards to involving the 47% that don't pay into the tax system to begin paying into it beyond pay roll tax. They must be invested in the process and the surest way to get someone to invest in something is through their pocketbook or wallet.

Economists will crunch numbers and come up with various results. They do that now with established mathematicians and economists. What I have attempted to put in this plan is ideas. My hope is that people, who are much smarter and well-versed in these issues, are examining all sides and discussing what is going to work best for our country. My goal is to simply put forth ideas from a layman's perspective in hopes something resonates. Across this great Land, there are millions like me who only pay attention to politics when things hit the fan. Otherwise we are trying to provide for our families and make a little difference in our small area of life. We rely on the "Big Shots" to come up with how to make things better for the individual. We concern ourselves with our homes and communities.

I have heard it said that America needs to wake up. I disagree. When I wake up in the morning it is a struggle. I slowly open my eyes and adjust to my surroundings. If there is an alarm clock sounding in the background I slowly lift myself out of the depths of my dreams and stumbling clumsily to shut the thing off. I usually do not fall back in the bed, but I know others that do. The next step is to sit on the side of the bed and assess my surroundings and figure out what I need to do to move forward. America doesn't need to wake up if it is anything like what I just described. America needs to already be up, to be awake. America needs to rise up and declare, through peaceful means that they, we, are tired of Washington as usual. There has to be leaders out there who can lead and get things done and reforming the tax code in this country can go a long ways towards restoring faith with the American people.

The last few years has left us disillusioned in many ways. The people we keep sending to Washington haven't gotten the job done. You have heard of the expression "keep your eyes on the prize." Well, the civil servants we have sent to Washington have sucked wind at this expression. I look at those running for office and those already there and I think, "Is that the best we've got?" It is pretty dismal to say the least. The American people are fed up. This book is full of like sayings and each time I write one I feel like it needs to be repeated more time than I have paper. The blaming of others is akin to third grade antics on the playground. No one would run their home or business like Washington runs our country. We want our politicians to perform and we need to hold them accountable.

You have heard me say repeatedly, that I am no economist or mathematician. I will be branded as some type of nut for my proposal by both sides of the political pundants. The Democrats will scream I am advocating for a tax hike on the 47% who don't pay federal taxes and on those in the middle class. The Republicans will argue that though the tax rate is lower, without the loop holes to take advantage of the deductions, I am raising taxes on small business because the business owners pay more in total tax. Both sides have valid points. We have to eliminate the loopholes. Loop- holes are a con to shape behavior and for the government to dictate behavior. If the rate is low enough, it won't really matter, and again, the goal for taxes is for them to decrease over time. As far as taxing the 47% it is correct too. Those more inclined to need help need to have some "skin" in the game and help with paying for services the federal government offers, especially in regards to National Security. All for one and one for all, right?

In the words of President Ronald Regan, "Government is not the solution to our problem. Government is the problem." (Reagan, 1981) As you will notice, I expect more revenue to be generated under my plan. Currently we take in about 2.5 or so trillion per year. We are currently about 1 trillion or so over budget. If we lower the tax rate and eliminate the deductions and require all to pay taxes then we can increase revenue to pay down our debt and fix the budgetary problems facing our country. Also, lowering the tax rate on the business sector will encourage more people to be hired which again, mean more people working and more revenue to the Government.

Chapter 3
Federal Agency Reform

"We must not let our rulers load us with
perpetual debt"

Thomas Jefferson, 1816

The Department of Education

The Department of Education was fully established in 1979. That was a short time ago. It has to do with control and is not essential to the three branches of government. While education is paramount and is the key to individuals rising up out of poverty it does not require federal oversight. The Department of Education needs to be eliminated. The federal government needs to send the collected allocation to the States. Each state in the union is capable of determining the needs facing its residents and how to effect growth. There is no need for a national standard or involvement. We do not need to restructure or reallocate employees or resources elsewhere. Cutting the Department of Education and eliminating the excess spending is the only conclusion when faced with the deep cuts facing our country! There will be many who argue this is going to be catastrophic for the people of this country. There is no evidence that is definitive on either side of the political parties to show federal involvement to the degree it is currently is needed to forward education across this great nation.

The United States of America is made up of states. We are united under the Constitution. We have, at our disposal 50 laboratories for experimentation to evaluate the methodology for success in our public school system. North Carolina, my home state, just went all in with Republicans in 2012. For the first time in forever we have a majority of Republicans in the House, Senate and in the Governor's mansion. The people of North Carolina decided to give Republicans a chance to put the people's money where the politician's mouth is. North Carolina needs to be watched closely by America. If these ladies and gentlemen serving the people do their conservative duty, America will see a prosperous and thriving economy in North Carolina. If they screw up this opportunity by making lazy, stupid decisions, then they won't get another shot like this for another 100+ years. Lead well Berger, Tillis and McCrory; America is watching.

Each of the fifty states wants people to move to their state. They want businesses to move to their state. They want their state to be showcased as the state with great growth opportunities. Competition is good. Let states and local people decide what bench marks are needed in their school(s), how to achieve success with their students and to showcase to the other states and to the world why their state is the best state to move to for business, to raise a family and to enjoy quality of life.

It is an accepted reality that teachers are pressured to teach students to take a test in North Carolina. The "No Child Left Behind Act" (Rotherham, 2007) had good intentions but it is an example of a Republican overstepping the bounds of the federal government. As it needs to be across the country, North Carolina and its people need to decide how to evaluate the success of our students. It is North Carolina and its people right to decide all the specifics down to being free to decrease or increase days and hours in the classroom. Everything needs to be up to the people at the local and state level in regards to educating its citizens. The goal of the federal government is to simply provide opportunity, so that all citizens, without discrimination, have an opportunity to gain a public education. How that is shaped, defined or evaluated is the responsibility of the individual state and local community within the union.

In giving each state the right to do as the state determines that is in the best interest of its citizens there needs to be no recoil or retaliatory response from the federal government. Teacher unions and other related public sector unions can be addressed, challenged and disbanded if the citizens within a state determine this is in their best interest. Tenure for teachers and other related "taboo rights" may be eliminated or reformed based on what the tax payers want to invest in. Again, the public school employee and all other public sector employees work for the tax payer. The tax payer is their boss and it is the tax payer who pays their salary.

Environment Protection Agency

We need to restructure the Environmental Protection Agency (EPA) and other related "red tape" agencies that have good intentions and offer safety and accountability, but exceed their authority and negatively impact the goal of growing businesses and the national / global economy. These programs were put in place, in part, because individuals and businesses were not doing a responsible job at taking care of our environment and other related areas of concern. Human nature is selfish. Government control is not the answer. Oversight, promoting job growth is appropriate, but oversight eliminating job growth is unacceptable. There is a way to provide accountability, oversight and insure appropriate safe-guards are being implemented without discouraging our economy's expansion.

The EPA needs to support current energy sources and reflect this in their policies. They also need to encourage the private sector to pursue alternative energy. The private sector will discover something eco-friendly and a product that can sale. The government does not need to discover this fuel and they don't need to throw money at it. It will come because investors and entrepreneurs will find a way. The Wright brothers in North Carolina out on the Outer Banks were not governmentally funded to find a way to fly airplanes. They did it because it was their passion and they dared to dream. Whoever thought we could send a hunk of metal into the sky and it would not only fly, but serve as a way to ultimately get to the Moon? I wonder if the Wright brothers sat on the sand dunes of Kitty Hawk and fantasized about flying to the Moon.

Until we discover alternative fuel that is cost efficient we need to drill on land, sea and wherever we can in this country to become energy independent. No longer do we need to depend on the Middle East for our oil or other governments who are repulsed by what the United States stands for. Who wants to go to a store and buy goods from an owner who hates the very sight of you? I can assure you, I would never continue going to a store of an owner who did not care for me and provide me with great service. If they despised America and the very values I hold dear to my heart, I sure as hell would not give them my money.

Develop nuclear energy and natural gas. Approve the Keystone Pipeline. This will bring jobs, economic growth and eliminate our dependence on energy from countries that hate us. We have tons of coal (Coal News, 2011). We have an enormous amount of natural gas (Hayes, 2012). We have oil. Just announcing we will drill and expand our mining for these resources will drop the price of current oil within six months. There is no reason not to do this. It is for the good of the country, the people and the security of our nation. Why this has not been done up to this point is a mystery? Reagan, Bush, Clinton, and Bush did not go all out and push us to energy independence. President Obama is not in favor of it either. One can speculate on the reasons, but for the life of me, I can't think of any one thing we could announce immediately that would have the greatest ripple effect throughout the world's economy than for us to seriously seek energy independence. The United States consumes twenty percent of the world's oil. America buys oil from countries, some, if not all, who don't like our way of life. If America announces to the world that we are pursuing energy independence and in ten years or so, we would no longer need to purchase oil from those countries, what do you think the ripple effect would be? Do you think it would change how these countries may treat America in regards of the price of oil? The price would drop to two dollars a gallon within six months. Why? These countries would want the price to drop so that America will delay drilling or seeking energy independence. However, they know we have a President who won't do that and does not believe in oil. They and the President have Americans over a barrel.

Internal Revenue Service

The Internal Revenue Services (IRS) needs to be eliminated by 75% or more due to the new tax code recommended in this book. A major overhaul of this Department is to happen. For one, the IRS has too much power over individuals. This is not the design of individual liberty. The idea an individual can be locked up and put in jail for not paying the government at the discretion of the IRS is scary. Simplifying the tax code means smaller government and less authority and size of the IRS. The reason this program has grown so much over the years is due to the filing and non-filing that goes on in this country. There is no reason for it. The new tax code introduced in the previous pages eliminates the need for this program and there carte blanche authority. Will there need to be oversight associated with the proposed tax collection plan? Yes. Can this be done with reduced cost and employees in the IRS department? Yes. Again, the federal government goal is to cut spending to needed levels. One of the biggest expenses for an entity is pay roll.

The downside discussed by some will be the effect taxes being taken out directly from pay roll and no need for filing and how that will impact the accounting business. It will hurt them. A lot of accountants make a good living off filing taxes for people. However, accountants are needed and they will bounce back and find their niche in another area of business need. Accountants are important and assist businesses evaluate their finances. There place in society and their ability to earn a good wage for their service will not perish. In fact, I would argue, it will increase in demand as more businesses need good, competent accountants to assist them with insuring their finances are on track. Again, the more the economy grows, the more everyone benefits.

Federal Reserve

The Federal Reserve needs accountability and auditing (Censky, 2012). Allow the federal government to borrow money for disaster or war until a saving(s) account fund can be appropriately accumulated. Borrowing can only come from the Federal Reserve and cannot exceed 35% of GDP at any time. There is no reason for the United States to borrow from other countries. Printing money only devalues the dollar and hurts us in the long run. We need to let the market work. We as a nation have to get to the point where we can sustain ourselves.

The scary thing is we can't sustain ourselves right now. We are in debt to nations that may or may not like us. They certainly don't have our best interest at heart like we do for our own citizens. Again, this is where my inexperience is an issue. I don't know how this all works, but I do know that currently it doesn't work for the best interest of the American people, their children, grandchildren and so on. Wallowing in debt is not a thriving nation and is counter to what America represents. Debt is a form of slavery. Anyone who has been in debt knows this feeling. It can lead to feelings of being stuck, controlled, and the understanding that your principles may be compromised at some point. It is a horrible feeling. Our nation is in this quick sand and we have to get out of this enslavement as soon as possible.

There are countless programs and areas of spending going on in the federal government to be carefully reviewed with funding evaluated.

Evaluation of each program has one of four outcomes: *cut, cap, reform and balance.* This should be the mantra for the next four years, but I don't believe President Obama believes we have a spending or debt issue. The changes needed won't happen over-night. It took time and patience along with a lot of indifference to get things as bad as they are financially in this country and it will take time, patience and a whole lot of intentionality to improve our condition. The American people expect results and frankly deserve better than what we have gotten. Think of all the waste throughout the years in regards to federal spending. Elected officials need to take notice and be given notice by the American people that it is time to "Put Up or Shut Up." This is especially important for the Republicans and why the Republicans need to be direct with the American people. Conservatives already can point to what liberalism and its failure brings. Making the Democrats continually push their agenda through without dealing seriously with the fiscal issues facing our country is good for conservatism. I don't see the Democrats reforming or cutting programs and their funding. The more focus and intentionality to these issues, the more effective are the results. No practical citizen truly believes there is unlimited funding, and if spending is not reined in then America suffers the same fate as those countries who tried similar spending sprees.

We need to pass an amendment that annual spending at the federal level needs to be 20% or less of GDP. There is no reason for the United States to spend more than three trillion or so annually on our budgetary needs. Does this mean I contradicted myself from the original 2.7 trillion or less budget mentioned earlier? No. The federal government is always to strive to live on the least amount possible. They owe that to the tax payer who pays the bills. If the government can do that on 2 trillion then it is 2 trillion. If the economy explodes and the GDP hits 22 trillion then technically the government budget would not exceed 4 trillion if we held at no more than 20% of GDP. That doesn't mean the government has to spend that much. If the new tax code generates 4 trillion annually then we pay our debt down earlier. The federal government also needs to reduce taxes as it can. For example, when we pay off our debt and have a government spending appropriately and all programs are sustaining themselves then the government goal is to reduce the amount taken from its employer. Remember, the government is owned by the people of the United States and not the other way around.

Outside of paying down the debt, which is where extra revenue needs to go every chance it is available, the annual budget needs to be no more than 2.7 trillion annually. The current growth rate of GDP is approximately sixteen trillion. In addition to this amendment, we need to add one in regards to the national debt.

There is no reason our national debt needs to exceed 35% of GDP. The other amendment to our Constitution is to require the federal government to balance its budget on an annual basis. Again, over the last few years, we have learned that spending can get out of control fast and to learn this lesson is one thing, but to insure it does not happen again requires making it more difficult to be this irresponsible again.

Another area recommended is to eliminate or greatly reduce pension plans for Congress, Senate and Presidents – this is a service. While these individuals supposedly work hard for their country, they have a lot of perks. Their package does not need to be better than what the average American worker is getting in the private sector. The idea of their benefits and retirement options being what they are is insulting to the Americans paying their salary. The idea that elected officials have some elite status in this regard perpetualates the notion of the Ruling Class which is the exact opposite of the founding fathers vision for our country.

In the 1995 movie Brave-heart, William Wallace, played by actor Mel Gibson (I know he is not the most beloved actor at this time) was speaking with the "nobles" after a victory over the wicked king, Longshanks, played by the wonderful Max Von Sydow. What initially was a victorious celebration appearing to unite the commoners and the nobles, turned into a feud with the nobles fighting amongst their respective clans for power!   Wallace and his men, the commoners, sadly turned to leave. As he was walking up the stairs to go out the door, the nobles stopped fighting with one another and one man yelled, "Where are you going, Sir William?" Wallace slowed his step, turned and gazed over the nobles who are literally below him. With all the nobles looking up at him Wallace responds, "You think the people of this country exist to provide you with position. I think your position exists to provide the people freedom. And I go, to make sure they have it."

This is so applicable in the American culture, right now. There is an elitist mindset that somehow the Ivy League graduate knows better than the rest of the Americans. When was the last time, a true commoner came along, who represented the people? There may be one out there I just don't know who it is. We hear the stories from all parties how they were poor once or they were this or that before going into elected office. No one is better than anyone and no one is above any other.

Socialism does not make an equal playing field. Socialism promotes stagnation and imprisonment of creativity. We are competitive beings. Just because competition brings out winners and losers doesn't mean it is wrong. In the movie, Brave-heart, the commoners had to want more for themselves than for the calculated compromise of the nobles. The commoners competed for freedom and were driven to be their own leaders and country. They were not interested in being ruled. They wanted freedom.

Socialism is a failed concept because it always ends in disillusionment. Its failure is smoldering around the globe. The economies of the world are on fire due to socialist-like policies. Conservatism, if presented in its most raw form, has a chance to change the course of history in a way that the founders could only dream. America needs its own William Wallace to rise up. Not in violence or war mongering, but in the battle of ideas leading the path to self-determination and achievement. Once the people of America digest the liberal, socialist policies designed to transform America they will cry out for the ideas of old because the old ideas work. Remember, a wheel is still a wheel no matter how old the concept is or how much it is seen on Nick at Night (Nation, 2012).

Federal Retirement

The federal retirement package needs to be revised. This needs to be what the private sector offers or less. Military personnel and other related national security operatives are an exception. No one working for the government is entitled to have a better benefit package then the hard working American paying the government employee salary (except those who put their lives on the line for our country). This is just another example of spitting in the face of the tax payer. We will discuss unions later, but the neighbor next door to the federal employee is paying their salary and the notion that somehow the federal employee deserves to be paid more or entitled to better benefits is lunacy. It would be no different than working at Wal-Mart and expecting the Walton family to earn less than the employee. How it got to this point is criminal; allowing it to continue is purely asinine.

Again the goal is to operate on 2.7 trillion or less on an annual basis. The government does not need to spend more than 2.7 trillion on its entire budget based on current needs. If anything, it needs to be under that amount. *Cut, Cap, Reform and Balance* is the mantra to progress and if the Republicans are smart they will do this until the Feds take in more than it spends. The United States has 4 battles. 1) those who hate our way of life and want to inflict harm to our citizens and country; 2) those who are trying to change or erase our Constitution and founding father's principles; 3) those who are against capitalism, which is similar to number two but can manifest differently; 4) national debt. The national debt is the one most pressing because the other three will always be there. There is no reason the national debt has to remain when we can do something about it in a definitive manner.

Chapter 4
Private Sector

"That some should be rich, shows that others may become rich, and hence is just encouragement to industry and enterprise. Let not him who is houseless pull down the house of another; but let him labor diligently and build one for himself, thus by example assuring that his own shall besafe from violence when built"

Abraham Lincoln, 1864

Unemployment Benefits

Eliminate the unemployment benefits program that employers are forced to pay into. Allow workers to get a policy from a private source (like short term disability) that can be called unemployment insurance. Individual workers can decide on how much coverage they want (6, 12 to 18 months). Insurance firms can establish criteria for what is an acceptable claim. This places the responsibility on the individual to provide the financial protection he or she is seeking. No employer needs to pay into a system that helps the unemployed. It is hard enough at times to pay for all the other elements that go into running a business.

Payroll Tax

Consider how to eliminate payroll tax for businesses once the new tax system has had time to operate and collect revenue. Set a time table for employers to be relieved of this responsibility. Again, we can't do it at the expense of spending more than we take in, but the goal needs to be to limit taxation as much as possible and to encourage job growth through expansion and hiring. Businesses are bombarded with taxes in an effort to stimulate the economy, but the reality is hiring more and more people produces more and more individuals paying into the economy. A person can spin it anyway he or she wishes, but this is an undisputed reality. The indicator of a healthy economy is taxation lessening over time.

As I stated earlier, small businesses make up the majority of the economic growth for this country (Longley, 2012). The focus is always on the wealthy or super rich, but the truth is there are not a lot of them in comparison to the rest of the population. Most business owners have money compared to the poor, but they aren't so well off they can just do whatever they want. Most small businesses are classified as individuals. This means, as stated above, they pay the whole 15% of the payroll. Look up the percentage the pay roll tax brings to the federal government and you will see it is close to 50% of the revenue (Williams 2011). Then look at the percentage of the federal revenue is from income tax and you will see that it is close to 50%. Keep in mind that 45% of the population does not pay federal income taxes. That is a large amount of money paid to the federal government and again, it doesn't include local and state taxes. The idea businesses aren't paying their fair share is a lie. In my plan, a self-employed individual who makes $200,000 annually pays 8% in federal income tax + 3% in national sales tax + 15% in pay roll tax. This totals to 26% to the federal government. That is a lot of money to the government no matter how you slice it.

Health Care Law

Repealing the Patient Protection and Affordability Care Act, otherwise known as

Obama Care, is probably not an option now, but it may be down the road. Just because it was put into place doesn't mean it can't be repealed, if it becomes as detrimental as the majority of Americans believe it to be. When the Health Care Law was "passed," the company I work for, which is a non-profit, received a call from their insurance representative. He informed our agency our cost was going up 50% within the month. In June of 2010, my cost went from $550+.00 per month for family coverage to over $830.00+ per month for the same exact coverage. The Agency I work for is only able to pay a certain percentage so my cost may be higher than some, but I believe the consensus across the country is health care premiums increased by approximately thirty percent.

This was a huge hit as a direct result of the passing of nationalized health care and the perceived costs associated with the law. I am certainly not an expert on the law by any means, but when the majority of Americans are not in favor of it and the majority of businesses owners are not in favor of it then one has to wonder the rationale for it. The costs associated with it continue to increase from the original 900 billion we were told it would cost. Again, the tax payer is the one footing the bills here. Government does not produce anything in and of itself.

The Supreme Court ruling was a huge blow to those who believe the health care law is unconstitutional. The court has a 5 to 4 conservative edge to it that typically leans to the right on constitutional issues. Chief Justice Roberts is considered a conservative and was expected to be the deciding vote to strike down the health care law. He surprised many by ruling it as a tax and therefore constitutional based on the 16th Amendment. I believe Justice Roberts ruling at the Supreme Court in June of 2012 was significant in two ways. The first is that it called the law a tax, which hurt the Democrat position of touting not raising taxes on the middle class and small business. The second thing the ruling did was demonstrate to the country the Court we look to, when all else fails, to uphold the Constitution, failed.

I don't know Chief Justice Roberts rationale for making his decision. Some believe Justice Roberts, a supposed constitutional conservative, was only upholding the government's ability to tax as stipulated in the sixteenth amendment. Some believe he was trying to put conservatives in a position to rise up and take the Senate and White House back so the health care law could be repealed. Some believe Justice Roberts wanted to avoid civil unrest by changing the language of the word "penalty" to a "tax" because to rule against the constitutionality of the law may provoke those in favor of the law to riot.

I have no idea of the complexities which is the refreshing part of writing this book. While I care and would love to understand more fully all the perspectives, in the end, what matters to me is the Constitution. The idea the federal government can mandate me, a citizen of the United States, to purchase a good or service I may or may not want to buy with my money, goes against every idea of the founding of this country. After all, the straw that broke the camel's back leading to the Revolutionary War was the excessive taxation and the taking of the individual's guns. Taking from others is stealing and the government is stealing from the people whom they work for.

If the government can demand a citizen purchase health insurance under the illusion of a tax then what else can it make an individual or business do next time? It is not that health care is bad, but it is not the federal government's role to tell me or you, the citizen and employer of the federal government, what to buy with the money we earn. Do you tell your boss what he is going to buy with his or her own money? Do your kids tell you what to do with your money that you work hard for? We are the owners of government and the boss of this country. The Supreme Court is to uphold the Constitution of this great country and everything is to be filtered through this prism without bias or prejudice. Again, I am only a layman, but I know enough to know this did not help get our fiscal house in order. Individuals were hurt. Business owners, who ironically are individuals, were hurt.

Health care has always been a huge expenditure for America. One of the many reasons (lawsuits among them) for this is the Emergency Medical Treatment and Active Labor Act (EMTALA) legislation passed in 1986 under President Ronald Reagan. This mandates all hospitals / Emergency Departments provide medical treatment for individuals who walk through their doors whether the individual can pay for services or not. Hospitals are prohibited under law to withhold services regardless of pay source. Hospitals can go after the individual in court to some degree to collect outstanding balances. If the hospital goes after payment too hard to collect outstanding balances from those who can't pay there may be ramifications for tying payment with services received.

It doesn't take a brain surgeon to figure out the cost for those who weren't insured were passed on to those who were insured which results in health care increasing at an alarming rate. It would be like going to McDonalds and paying $39.95 for a Quarter Pounder meal. You ask to see the manager and she informs you the price is that high because there are individuals who come through their doors who can't pay and therefore McDonald's has to provide their meal for free. The cost is passed on to the consumer who pays in an effort to help everyone. While this is a nice gesture, it only encourages irresponsibility and places the financial burden on those being responsible with their money.

The national health care law is not going to fix the problem. We are stuck with it because of a poor Supreme Court ruling. We are stuck with it because of how it was passed through Congress in 2010. We are stuck with it because the conservatives did not turn out and support Governor Romney for president. Just remember, health care was passed on to the federal government because of the ever rising cost and its impact on society. So, we in America believe the Federal Government, who is irresponsible beyond words with our money, will somehow demonstrate financial responsibility with one of the greatest expenditures of our time. Yeah, that will go well.

There are many ways to drive cost down and still provide quality health care coverage to those who want to purchase it. Open up insurance companies to bid across state lines. Allow portability. Employers don't need to offer insurance to their employees. Individuals need to purchase their own health care policy. This goes back to individual responsibility. Increase competition and thereby drive the cost down for the consumer. As a consumer, I should be able to purchase a health care policy for me and my family that works for us. If I see a health care plan from a company based in Seattle, Washington I should be able to purchase it. Individuals should be able to go through various health care plans and add what they want and take off what they don't want. It should work similar to signing up for Direct TV or related cable package or purchasing a car at a dealership. Get what you want, from where you want that works best for you. Can you imagine going on-line to order something, but informed you can only purchase something offered in the state in which you reside. That is ridiculous and anyone with half a brain knows this when they think about it in that way.

Another option worth considering is the establishment of Health Care Savings Accounts or HSA. This is where individuals put their own money into an account; tax free, to be used for medical expenses throughout their life. If the federal government wanted to be bullish, they could mandate individuals participate, but the difference would be the individual would control the investment and the money. There are options that promote responsibility.

Unions

Address union(s) and the ability of states to become Right to Work states or to greatly reduce the bargaining rights of unions that cripple businesses – at least as it impacts government related unions. Chicago is a great example. In 2012, the teacher union is essentially demanding that they won't work unless their neighbor pays them more. Children are being held hostage and there is no way for the law markers there to say "We won't make deals. You all are out of work and we are bringing in new teachers from across the country, who will work." Employers, in this case are the tax payer, need to have the right to hire and fire based on performance and other related criteria and need not be dictated to by the employee. If a privately held company wants to allow union activity then that is on that business, but it does not need to be the right of the unions to simply dictate to the business. On top of all of this, employees need to have unrestricted rights to not join unions or pay union dues. It is ridiculous to hear about automatic deductions from employee pay checks to union dues simply because the person works in a union- run area.

Subsides

Eliminate government subsidies to most endeavors. There may be some value in some assistance, but for the most part the government needs to get out of it. Defining what is absolutely necessary and what is not will get messy because everyone with a stake in these subsidies will want their slice of the pie. While there will be no agreed upon consensus on the issue – it has to be dealt with and a decision made. Allow the market to dictate. The federal government needs to stick to a budget that does not exceed 2.7 trillion and if at all possible make enough cuts and/or restructure programs so that the budget is less than 2.7 trillion. The budget may grow by three to five percent annually after 4 years of staying at 2.7 trillion. Again, money spent belongs to tax payers and no one else. Every single area that federal money is spent needs to be examined closely to determine if it is truly necessary and if so, why? If the program funding cannot be legitimately supported as being essential then it needs to be reduced or eliminated.

For example, Agricultural Subsides may be a great assistance to farmers (Edwards, 2009). The oil companies will argue that subsidies coming to them help out as well. The argument from all is that it eventually filters down to the common man, not the wealthy businessman, and therefore it is desperately needed and without it, the individual, community and surrounding area will be devastated. This will be contrasted with others stipulating that the other is taking advantage of the tax payer and they don't need the assistance. It goes around and around. The politicians do the safe thing and kick the can down the road. The road is at a dead end. There is no room for kicking anymore. Now, everyone seems to kick each other because there is no more Road for kicking the can. It is ridiculous. Subsidies need to be examined closely and decided upon based on absolute need. No more blame. No more spin.

Chapter 5
The Social Net

"I am for doing good to the poor, but I differ in opinion of the means. I think the best way of doing good to the poor, is not making them easy in poverty, but leading or driving them out of it"

Ben Franklin, 1776

Social Programming

Imagine you see a person on the street corner who is asking for help. You see the sign and sympathize with his plight. You pull the car over, get out and strike up a conversation with the individual. You hear his story about losing his job and trying to feed his family. He comes across as genuine and you invite him to go with you to have a bite to eat. He accepts. You find he appears sincere and you think, "I could be like this one day if things got bad." You decide to give him some money and give him some contacts for possible jobs. He thanks you and you feel good about your efforts. The next week you drive by and see the same man holding a sign in the same location. You don't have time to stop, but you offer up a prayer and keep going. A few weeks later you drive by and there he is again. You stop and reacquaint yourself with the man holding the sign. You ask him how things are going and what happened with the follow up information you gave him. He says he doesn't have a phone and could not get to the employers office. It seems plausible. You offer him your phone and he calls the would-be employers. You take him to eat and give him more money. Again you drive home feeling satisfied, but a question begins to linger in your mind about the man's interest in working a job. You dismiss it and feel bad for thinking it.

Over the course of months you see the same guy out on the same street holding a sign indicating he will work for food and he wants a job. You have stopped many times and each time you are met with an excuse on why he hasn't followed up with leads offered him. You feel good about your efforts to help, but not about his efforts to help himself. Finally, you stop one last time and strike up a familiar conservation with the man. He seems glad to see you and ask if you are taking him to grab some dinner. Reluctantly you take him to eat. You stall through the meal having small-talk to avoid a confrontation at the diner. On the way back, you decide to speak to him directly at the street corner once he is outside of your car. You ask him "What is your deal? I have offered help each time I could stop. I have given you contacts and taken you for meals. Why do you live this way?" The man responds calmly "Why don't you like my lifestyle. I have people like you stop every day and give me help. It gets me by and that is all I want." You respond by saying, "But your sign. It says you want help. You want to work." The man smiles and says, "I am working. I log a lot of hours out here attracting people like you. It gets people to help me. They feel sorry for me and it makes them feel better to help someone like me. It works like a charm. You are living proof. Thanks for all your help, but I guess you won't be stopping by anymore." You walk away disillusioned. You try to make sense of it and it just doesn't add up. Why would anyone settle for medicrocity when he could strive for more?

The story above doesn't represent everyone receiving assistance from the federal government. I would estimate only 30% of the people on assistance actually are cheating the system intentionally. At the same time, I would say another 30% are enslaved to the assistance program without truly grasping how much better life would be if they strived for more, but have settled for living off the hand-out. Safety nets are great and needed. I am not necessarily for the federal government providing the safety net, but in this day and age, that concept won't change completely. What can change is the way in which assistance funding is provided to the individual.

Webster's definition for the word "entitlement" is: a right to benefits specified especially by law or contract. The concept of entitlement programming is great. Politicians are famous for citing Contracts with America. Entitlements got started this way and continue on due to this ideology. The problem is twofold.

The cost is the biggest issue and what America spends annually on entitlements and social programming is unsustainable. Entitlements are contracts and need to be reformed, but they represent a contract with the individual who is paying into the system. It is not a hand out. People can argue that the individual gets a bigger return over the course of their life off Medicare, but they get swindled on Social Security.

The other issue is social programing. Social programs are not contracts with the individual based on my opinion and don't involve the individual actually paying into the program. Social programing involves the process where people are no longer responsible for themselves. Now there are those who need the safety net and sincerely cannot care for themselves. This is not the majority. I would estimate one-third either is cheating the system and the other third need help for a short-time, but could become self-sufficient. Medicaid,

Food Stamps and other related social programs need to be programs that offer assistance in addition to the person's efforts to help themselves and not in spite of their lack of effort. It also needs to be time limited with no more than a 6, 12 or 18 month window of assistance.

Consider this story to illustrate a point. A little ten year old girl was asked by the local paper what she wanted to do when she grew up. This little girl had raised $150.00 for a local homeless shelter in the area and she was being interviewed for such patriotism. The little girl explained she wanted to help the poor and make a difference. The reporter asked the little girl what she was going to contribute to this travesty. She said she was going to raise more money. The reporter pressed the little girl about what she was going to do personally to help. She explained how she was making money by doing her chores and even had a baby sitting job recently for a neighbor. The reporter again asked the little girl how much she was going to give of her money to help those who were hungry. The little girl looked puzzled and sheepishly asked, "If I can make my own money to buy things, why can't those who are poor do the same?"

While people need help sometimes, dependency is never the answer for those who can otherwise care for their own needs. Providing long-term support or blanket support to individuals is not healthy for the individual and their family. It conveys disrespect and lacks value in the belief of the person to rise up and aspire for greater things. It promotes an attitude in the culture that the "have-nots" simply can never have and need to be cared for by those who "have." Who believes he or she cannot achieve? Who is dreamless? What kind of society props people up on a crutch and sends the message, "You will always need this crutch and you will never be whole." The system needs to be reformed and the language the system communicates to Americans needs to inspire and lift up those fighting to survive. It needs to deliver a resounding song of hope to the heart of the human condition conveying "Here is a little help, but you are too valuable to our society to be depended on it. Rise up and pursue your dreams. We need you."

Food Stamps

In America, we have approximately 47 million people on Food Stamps (Cox, 2012). This has increased every year for the last four years. The Food Stamps program needs to be reduced to supply no more than 18 months of help. After that, people need to plug into local communities for help. The goal is for people to be off Food Stamps and federal assistance, not survive on it. As a therapist, clients coming for therapy generally seek help because they are having difficulties. That may sound like a no-brainer, but there are those who go to therapy for no other reason than to just talk to someone.

I know of people who have been seeing their therapist for years. If you have to see the same therapist for years and you don't have a significant diagnosis warranting this with medical oversight involved too, then I would submit the individual has become codependent on the therapist. Once this happens the professional is propping up the individual and interfering with his or her ability to become self-determined and reclaim their life. People engage in behaviors because they can. Obstacles in behavior change ultimately come down to two reasons: 1) the person cannot change because he or she does not possess the skills and/or abilities or 2) the person refuses to change, whether there is a justifiable reason from his or her perspective or not. It really is this simple in the majority of cases. Very few individuals lack the ability for change. The majority waffle between wanting to change, but not willing to put the work into the change to produce the supposed stated outcome. The real key to change is adverse stimuli. Change occurs when the pain of staying the same exceeds the pain of change. The individuals receiving Food Stamps need to be reviewed to determine: Does the person need Food Stamps long term or does the person needs short-term help?   If it is the later, then measures need to be put in place to titrate the individual off the support?   Once the person is placed in the proper category then a determination needs to be made to time the ones out that possess the ability to work, but just don't want to for a variety of reasons.

There is no one in this country who believes those individuals who cannot truly feed themselves or care for other needs are to be cut off and left to fend for themselves. It is absurd to entertain such rhetoric. The bottom line is the majority receiving food stamps need it as a jump start to propel them to self-dependency. It is a safety net for the majority, but not a way of life. The exclusion is for those who cannot, for identified rational reasons, provide for themselves in the way of calorimetric intake. These folks need to be identified and connected with State services and other related options within their state to insure they receive the care they need. An educated guess on my part would put the percentage of people needing this level of care and intervention at about 30% of the Food Stamp population. The rest, I would imagine, can benefit from 12 to 18 months maximum of assistance from the federal government in regards to Food Stamps.

The other thing to consider, now that America is trending in the direction of liberalism, is it won't be long before the federal government proposes to provide everyone with meals and groceries through a mandated Food Stamp system. It will be similar to the health care law which is really designed to help those without insurance and not the ones who already have insurance. There are 47 million on Food Stamps and it will keep on growing (Kurtzleben, 2012). Remember, there are only 30 million without insurance and look what happened.

It won't be long before someone starts making headlines on the need to feed all Americans because food is a basic life right. Day Care will be on the table at some point. College funding has been discussed over the years. Ultimately, the way power is kept is through permission and the people will only surrender their rights if they perceive the alternative landscape is just too hard. The end game is power for Democrats. Democrats stay in power by giving gift bags and goodies to the commoners while discrediting the opposition. You can dress it up however you like, but if the gifts stop coming, the power goes to the other side. If the economic climate blows up and our economy collapses, the people will look elsewhere.

Think of it this way, a teenager or young adult who gets what he or she wants is fine as long as that selfishness within is continually fed. Once the parents start standing up to the demands by putting limits in place, things usually get ugly pretty quickly and the teenager turns on the parents. The problem with the analogy is the American People are the parents of government and the elected officials are the teenagers instructed on how to conduct themselves by the people. Somewhere along the way, through sleight-of-hand, these roles have switched and the country is suffering for it.

Medicaid

Medicaid is a social program. Medicaid recipients come in three forms. 1) Those who can't fend for themselves and need Medicaid to access related health needs 2) Those who need help for a short period of time (12 to 24 months), but are trying to get back on their feet and be self-determined 3)Those who are taking advantage of the system. Maybe they need short-term help initially, but due to loopholes in the system they have stayed on the Medicaid rolls for years.

There are adults out there who are getting disability assistance and Medicaid because they have Attention Deficit Disorder or Bi-Polar Disorder or they hurt their foot and yet walk just fine. I have seen it in Emergency Departments. It is amazing the various ways there are to seemingly take advantage of this program. Some may argue that individuals taking seemingly advantage of the program are committing fraud and need to be reported. I am sure there is a way to report fraud, but to report fraud on "appearance of" with no substantial supporting documentation is not going to stand up in court. Besides, there is probably a loop hole validating their claim.

Medicaid does serve a role in society, especially among kids. No one, not even conservatives, are in favor of dumping kids off Medicaid and leaving kids without health insurance. No one is advocating kids / adults with autism, Down's syndrome or related disabilities that impair their ability to self-care in society to go without Medicaid. It is the people out there who can work, who can care for themselves, but find it easier to live off the dole of the American tax payer that take money away from those who need it. One way of controlling cost is to eliminate the Medicaid department in Washington and send money to the state(s) to distribute as block grants to their respected counties. This would control cost, put states responsible for administering and overseeing it and create 50 laboratories out there to see who can actually fix the problem and still provide for those who need it.

Medicaid is needed in some form. I don't know if Medicaid in its current form is the right way. What I do know is Medicaid is a local issue and not a federal issue. States need to be in control of this money without restriction or accountability from the federal government. The money came from its citizens and is for the state's citizens. Who else is better at looking out for the citizens in this area than the local government? Who better knows the need of its citizens than the citizens in that state? It's not the politicians. It's the citizens.

As mentioned above, children and those who can't care for themselves are the ones to be covered by Medicaid. I work with an agency serving children and families who have Medicaid and need treatment for mental health disorders. In the state of North Carolina, there is a ton of programming even though most professionals in my field may disagree with me. Just in the child/adolescent area of mental health there is a program to fit almost any client needing mental health services and is on Medicaid. Not true for those with private insurance. In my field, those with private insurance cannot access the same services as those with Medicaid. While there is a methodology to access funding for these families, in reality these accounts are bankrupt and do not provide any real assistance to families not on Medicaid without a lot of hoop jumping.

I know health professionals who only treat private pay clients and the attendance of these families following through on appointments is outstanding. The reason is if they miss the appointment then the person is billed for the missed session. This same approach cannot be implemented with Medicaid patients. Charging a Medicaid patient for a missed appointment is illegal. However, Medicaid patients in my field, and I understand it is the same in other places, have a thirty percent or higher "no-show" rate on appointments. They may want to get better, but their investment in the treatment lacks the responsibility and effort needed to make the gains needed to improve their ability to cope with the stressors in their life. Not all is due to lack of investment, but a large portion of it is and most professionals, if they are honest, will verify it.

Medicaid **IS** free health care for those on it. Hospitals and other health agencies become a revolving door for those on it. Again, there is a percentage currently on Medicaid that needs this service. There are those who cannot care for themselves and need the service. However, there is approximately 30 to 40 percent who don't need the service or if he or she does, they need it for a limited time rather than using it for years on end. There has to be measures put in place to reduce the roles and eliminate those folks who take advantage of it, while providing for those who need it. Sending the money to the States is the best way to do this with zero interference from the federal government.

The block grant for social programming/health care ideology has been around for years. I don't know how it fits together, but it seems to me the social programming money going back to the states for the resident, cuts out the middle-man, aka the federal government, and puts the money closer to the hands of the American people. Here is the short and sweet.

Decide how much each state within the Union needs to care for the people. This block grant would be used for: Medicaid, Education, Health Care and other related programming. Insure portability so coverage and support is valid across state lines for health care related issues. As an example, North Carolina may need 23 Billion annually. California may need 200 Billion annually. If each state / territory received the amount below then each state / territory would be equipped to care for all their people's need and save money in the process by reducing the size of the federal government. This is in addition to what the individual state taxes its residents. The amounts below may not be enough. What would it take? How much better are the states at knowing and caring for their residents?

California has the most people and the most problems. There issues are largely due to their own making. However, I don't want to bash individual states so in staying with the train of thought mentioned above, the federal government can just give 200 billion annually to California. Texas can receive 63 billion and New York and Florida can both receive 48 billion. Illinois, Pennsylvania can receive 31 billion while Ohio receives 29 billion. Michigan, Georgia and North Carolina can receive 23 billion while New Jersey and Virginia will receive 22 billion. Washington, Massachusetts, Indiana, Arizona, Tennessee and Missouri will receive 16 billion and Maryland will receive 15 billion. Wisconsin will receive 14 billion, and Minnesota will receive 13 billion as well as Colorado with 13 billion. Alabama, South Carolina, Louisiana and Kentucky will receive 10 billion. Oregon, Oklahoma, Connecticut and Iowa will receive 9 billion. Mississippi, Arkansas, Kansas, Utah,

Nevada, New Mexico will receive 7 billion. West Virginia, Nebraska, Idaho, Hawaii, Maine, New Hampshire, Rhode Island, Montana, Delaware, South Dakota, Vermont, Washington D.C., Wyoming, North Dakota will all receive 5 billion. America territories like Guam, Virgin Islands, A. Samoa, North Mariana and Puerto Rico will receive 1 billion each.

The total above comes out to 907 billion of annual giving from the federal government that was taken initially from the tax payer and invested back into each of the fifty states. Again, I don't like giving the Feds more than what is needed, but if the money was ear-marked for the states then the above has possibilities. It certainly emphasizes local control. If the federal government sent the tax payer dollars back to the states and allowed them to use it to provide quality Medicaid, health care, education, disaster relief and other related social programs would not the above funds be a good start? I know in North Carolina that our state takes in about 20 billion dollars. Receiving another 23 billion to care for its residents seems like enough. I don't know what the feds send North Carolina in regards to additional funding. Most records indicate it is around thirty percent of the state budget. It may exceed the amounts above. I know states are better at knowing what their residents need and how to make their state grow. The more localized assistance programs are the more accountability can be delivered. Again, it is just an idea. If it adds cost then it is probably not a good idea, but if it saves cost in the long run by reducing the size and scope of the federal government, then maybe that returns more control to the states...and to the people.

Social Security

Social Security is an entitlement and not a social program from my perspective. This is an account an employee paid into for years in agreement with the United States he or she is going to get a return on their investment to help with retirement. Again, entitlements are contracts, not hand-outs. There is a difference and Republicans need to make the distinction to the American people. The media has long lumped entitlements in with social programs and Republicans have let this happen. These programs are different and Republicans need to work hard at clarifying the difference. As far as reforming Social Security, here are suggestions.

The first is to increase the Social Security retirement age to 75 in 2018. Start this for those under 45 years of age in 2018. People are living longer and working longer. Allowing individuals to draw into their account later in life is not unreasonable and still provides for them in the later stages of their life. The second option is to do the above while implementing this 2nd step. Eliminate the current process for individuals less than 20 years of age in 2018. The idea of allowing individuals to control their investment has been around for a long time.

The idea that the government has the right to tax a person and invest it for them and then decide when the person can receive what the person himself earned is a loan-shark mentality. It flies in the face of the Constitution. However, my goal is to not to completely eradicate the system, but to offer possible solutions that may be embraced in today's world with today's leaders.

There are many options to privatizing Social Security and assuring Americans their money won't be lost in a Ponzi scheme. Mine is my own without outside influence that I know of, but again most good things are plagiarized at some point. Since the government wants to control the individual, strike a compromise that works for the individual. Require individuals to save 7 to10% (he or she can save more) of each pay check and place it into a savings program of their choosing for that individual to grow it for retirement. This money automatically comes out, but is designated to a specific fund or account decided on by the Individual. A company can make a match if the company wants. It would elevate the expense businesses have in matching the payroll tax each pay period that companies are required to do for their employees.

The requirement would be to put 7 to 10% into the IRA, mutual fund or related retirement program options. A person may not draw on it for any reason until he or she turns 59 years of age. No penalty is associated with drawing on it at 59 and a person can make as much as he or she can earn while drawing off their retirement savings. It is their money. They can will it to anyone if they die. They can give it to someone if they choose. They can do with it what they want because, are you ready, it's their money.

Again, having people save for retirement is good. Most people fail to plan, so if this is the way the government wants to show how much it cares and looks after its people, then there is very little down side to this approach. All the same precautions are in place. The individual has to participate. There is no opting out. The individual has to save a designated minimum amount and can't have access to it. The funds are automatically transferred, so there is a guarantee it will happen or the employer will face federal violations.

The problem with this concept is that the government wants access to the money in Social Security. It has very little to do with helping the individual prepare for retirement. It is about access. If Social Security is privatized with specific safe-guards in place to protect the individual, the Left still will not embrace it. At some point the American people have to ask "How can the individual having complete control and access to their money, be bad policy for the individual?" Again, the principle of saving for retirement is sound. If the majority of the people want this process to be forced upon them by the government, to insure they, the American people, do the responsible thing and save for their own future; then what is described above may be embraced by the majority of the people. The politicians may be a different matter.

There are great minds out there and I leave it to them to figure out the specifics, but the bottom line is the government has a goal to assist people plan for their future when they retire. While I think this is wrapped up in power and control, the program is not going to go anywhere anytime soon. Conservatives have a hard time with the government taking any money from individuals and I get that, but I also know that structure and discipline create freedom. I fundamentally disagree with mandating a person save a percentage of their check towards retirement or be required to pay the excessive taxes Americans are forced to pay. However, if the people want it and it lessens the possibility the individual will need to be cared for by the tax payer, then I can support some form of it.

The accounts can be carefully selected with tight accountability on the Hedge Fund Investors. The government could evaluate investment companies based on integrity and financial sustainability to insure those selected to fund this operation will take care of the tax payer's money. I don't know all the accounts out there, but there is Vanguard, Fidelity and others that may have decent track records with little criminal history. The goal is to avoid a Bernie Madoff scenario. Remember, in our current system, if a person dies he loses his money. It may go to their kids for a while or their spouse can decide if he or she wants the bigger check or not, but there are strings attached by the government on an American's money. Giving the individual more access and control over their money may promote Americans to force elected officials to compromise for the good of each American.

A compromise won't happen with Liberals and Conservatives on this matter without the pushing of the people. There is too much money at stake for the Liberals. This program needs transformation and since elimination will never occur a transformation is a victory for the individual. It needs to be returned to the individual to promote choice and more control of their money. Again, this mandate is there to insure people save, but how they save, where they save it and how much they earn after they tap into it and who is given the money that is left over is none of the government's business.

Medicare

Medicare is an entitlement program to our seniors to help them with medical related expenses as they grow older. This program is a contract with seniors and is a program individuals count on to off-set costs associated with retirement. The problem, if you can call it that, is people are living longer than when the program was initially conceived. Health care costs have dramatically increased. Life is just much more expensive and the longer a person lives the more it costs. My recommendation is simple. Change the age to receive Medicare to 75 years of age. Enforce these changes for those 45 years or younger in 2018.

The more extreme recommendation I would love to see implemented is the elimination of Medicare in its current form for those 18 years of age and younger beginning in 2018. Remember, these are the individuals who are required to save 7 to 10% out of each check towards retirement based on my recommended change to Social Security. Have these same individuals save an additional 2% towards Health Care Costs for retirement (or it can be incorporate into their HSA discussed earlier). This is tax free when drawn on in retirement and is strictly to be there to provide an off-set for the individual in regards to medical expenses. This plan puts the ownership on the individual. It is automatically taken out of each check. The individual cannot draw on it until he or she is fifty-nine years of age. However, the individual controls all aspects of the investment and can leave it to his or her heir if he or she so chooses.

Again, this may not be embraced by conservatives, but the goal is for the individual to keep their money. There is everything wrong with "forced savings." I don't disagree. I just realize deals have to be made and if a deal can be struck that allows for the same end result, but the individual maintains control of their earned money, then it is worth consideration. We all know the true goal of government is to thrive and the way to thrive is to take the individual's money. A good test for the people is to watch closely who is opposed to recommendations like mine? Who is it that believes the individual can't control his or her own investment? Who is it that eloquently speaks of the government being irresponsible if the government placed this investment burden on the individual? When the people witness this double-speak; may they rise up; not in violence, but in a revolution of peaceful demonstration at the voting box.

Federal Government School Loans

Why is the tax payer paying for people to get loans through the federal government? Revise government loans for financial aid. Encourage banks and lenders to charge no more than 4% in interest for those who qualify. Allow lenders to decide who qualifies based on debt ratio. If you can't afford a loan and are not a good risk to pay it back based on debt ratio or history, etc then lenders have responsibility to decline your application. Make sure it is clear that minorities and other related lower income or disadvantaged persons must qualify for the loan based on numbers that don't discriminate and insure that the press and others can't make this debate stick about it being discriminatory towards people. It is only discriminatory towards people who don't manage their money well or have no collateral to offer to offset the risk. Government does not need to being loaning out money that is not theirs so people can go to college. This is not the federal government's role. Insure opportunity is out there so people can get an affordable loan if they want it, but don't get in the way of the lender being able to accurately discriminate based on a person's ability to pay the loan back. If state institutions want to offer assistance, then that is something for the local leaders to work out, but not the federal government.

One main area the federal government may consider looking into are public universities and college where the cost of getting a degree keeps going up while the economy remains on life support. Public institutions get a lot of money from the government to operate. Most have endowments to offset what they need to provide quality education. While private institutions can charge what they like, public institutions need to be capped. I am not sure how I feel about the government's involvement or funding of these endeavors to begin with, but if they are going to be involved at public institutions, the government needs to control the cost for the student. There is no reason, at a public institution offering a four year degree that the tuition and cost of the education per year need to exceed four thousand dollars. The school makes money on volume, the federal and state government (tax payer) and their endowment program (alumni). Yes, these institutions prepare minds to enter the work force and contribute to society, but these institutions in and of themselves don't produce anything. I can hear it now. "He said, college does not produce anything and therefore is a waste of time and money." No, I am not inferring college is worthless or does not benefit society.

On the contrary, it was of great value to me when I went to school in many ways. There is direct correlation between those who earn a four degree and being able to live above the poverty line. However, debt is no one's friend and if a student is racking up massive debts while earning their degree then he or she is at a disadvantage when he or she graduates. Also, just because college and graduate school are important, this path is not the only path to take in life. There are plenty of successful people who did not graduate college. While education is important, it is not essential. What is essential is working. What qualities are essential are drive, ambition and achievement. These qualities are instilled before college in most cases and point to a person's character. Without education the people will still find a way to invent products, start businesses and hire people. Without entrepreneurs, the economy stops. There is a big difference between the two entities.

Housing Market

Government needs to get out of the way of the housing market. Allow lenders to qualify prospective buyers based on legitimate criteria as it relates to debt ratio and ability to competently pay back the loan. Again, no one in America needs to be approved for a loan (car and/or house) that is in debt 26 to 30% or more of their gross income. If the government can conservatively participate in providing accountability towards this goal, while not dictating to the private sector, then appropriate rules need to be put in place. Again, accountability is important and all need accountability, but the government does not need to be in charge. People are accountable to self and others – not to government. Government is accountable to the people.

The housing crash can be traced back to both Republicans and Democrats (Hancock, 2011). However, it doesn't take a brain surgeon to evaluate the cluster frig and determine that somewhere, someone put in place something that allowed all people to buy a house. Whether they could afford it or not was not the point. The point was probably some form of supposed identified discrimination that excluded those with low income not being able to afford to buy a house. *Banks do discriminate and it is important to note it. It is based on color. The color is green.* Banks want to make money and could care less what race a person is or where he or she is from for that matter. Banks like to make loans because they like to make money. Banks do not like to lose money. Remember, their goal is to make money. In order to figure out who is a good bet to invest in and who is not a good risk the banks discriminate based on a person's income, debt ratio and ability to pay the loan back as stated in the contract. Nothing more is involved from the bank's perspective. Politicians made it more complicated than it needed to be and the people got hurt. It is important to note that none of the elected officials involved in the housing market fiasco are hurt by it. None of them lost their house. Sometimes the enemy of the best is the good. There is a good reason why everyone can't buy a house. The federal government needs to get out of the way of business. It can't even pass a budget, let alone balance one. Who are they to direct business practices?

Chapter 6
National Security

"`Deterrence' means simply this: making sure any adversary who thinks about attacking the United States, or our allies, or our vital interests, concludes that the risks to him outweigh any potential gains. Once he understands that, he won't attack. We maintain the peace through our strength; weakness only invites aggression"

Ronald Reagan, 1983

Department of Defense

The Department of Defense needs to be able to operate on 400 – 600 billion per year with salary advances and needed equipment factored into this over the next 8 years. This needs to include any "War on Terror" spending. We need a strong military. We need to be proactive at insuring our military has what it needs at all times. We need to care for our Veterans. We also need accountability and discipline when it comes to fiscal responsibility. It is too easy to make headlines about pro-military issues to lay off dealing with military spending. This is a sticking point for many liberals and it needs to be addressed within reason, to take the topic off the table or at least offset the combativeness that is often associated with military spending.

"Show of Strength" does work. Think about when you see a policeman in your rearview mirror or you see multiple law enforcement officers at a particular event.

People become more mindful of their behavior. The United States military serves the same function. We don't have to go to war so much as demonstrate we can go to war. We need to practice relentless training exercises to show case the latest ways we can obliterate a nation off the map. Passive strategies usually don't work. Sure Ghandi and Dr. King made changes with their peaceful protest. However, protest is different from war and America does have enemies and our enemies want to kill us. Our enemies need a very clear and loud message that shouts, "Mess with the bull and you get the horns."

The biggest problem I have with the military is the restraints politicians place on their respective units. We don't allow them to take the gloves off and fight. It's like having a fire department respond to a fire with people trapped inside and telling the fireman, "Hey, just contain the blaze. Let the building and people burn. Don't put it out, just offer support." A fireman is going to look at you like you have lost your mind unless there is an absolute reason for this directive that makes logical sense to them in the way they were trained. Otherwise, what is the point of firemen being there if they can't do their job?

It is the same with the military. They aren't police who are trained to protect and only use force in certain situations. The military is trained to kill. They are trained to eliminate the opposition without discrimination. When one considers the way terrorists fight, it is difficult to figure out who are the civilians and who are the terrorists. The terrorists use civilian's homes and use them as shields (Cooper & Brackman, 2009). We take the "noble" way out and end up getting our soldiers dead. We police the world and our soldiers die. This is inexcusable. If the United States needs to go to war, then we need to take the gloves off our fighting men and women and let them do their job. Again, the point to war is to kill and thereby bring the enemy into submission in hopes of conquering the enemy and ending the war. Political correction and niceties have no place in combat.

"Show of Strength" is also about Intelligence. Gathering information, developing assets and knowing the real players is gold to properly planning how to execute our military offensive. Yes, the military is designed to kill and eliminate. It is also about performing in a smart and efficient way resulting in minimal casualties on our side. Designing and implementing systems communicating and collaborating with identified agencies to properly prepare our military for possible strikes is essential. We need more of this approach and continued use of enhanced interrogation techniques and the like to insure we are getting the information we need when we need it. We need to continue to have assets in other countries providing quality and useful information. We need to insure all aspects of these agencies are working in concert with one another so we can respond quickly, decisively from a position of strength.

In regards to showing strength, it means the military has to have access to the latest technologies and equipment upgrades. People get so upset with the amount the federal government spends on Defense and compare it to federal spending on Education. The two are completely different. The Constitution clearly states the role of the federal government is to protect and defend the United States. By showing a clear advantage in strength and dominance, we minimize the chance of going to war with other nations. There is something powerful seeing and knowing there are American aircraft carriers at sea around the world, seeing airplanes take-off these massive ships. It is powerful knowing that lurking under the waters there are nuclear submarines out at sea. We need more of them, but fiscal responsibility comes first.

The recent September 11, 2012 attack on our embassy in Benghazi, Libya is an example of poor political leadership. I am not on the inside of things in Washington and I admit; I am just a small town voice from the great state of North Carolina. I have no military experience, no research experience in the area of military, but what I do have, is the great respect and admiration for the brave men and women who protect us day in and day out. There is argument over what leadership knew and what they did with what they knew. Remember, "Peace through Strength." We had Americans in harm's way in a hot spot area of Libya known for terrorism and recent attacks. Great Britain removed their Ambassador this past summer after derailing an assassination plot slated against him.

Communications were sent from Libya to Washington, where they were most likely received in the Situation Room in the White House among other places (Griffin & Housley,

2012). There is someone watching for these cables and as soon as an alert comes through the secure channel he or she takes the transcripts to the Watch Commander (WC). The WC then takes the alert to the Decision Maker in the White House to receive orders on how to proceed. My guess is this is drilled on so much that when it happens, it is second nature to those monitoring the traffic. There is no way no one knew what was going on and there is no way there was too much "chatter" on the wire to discern what was accurate. None of this makes any sense. We have units on stand-by around the globe for extraction missions. We had to have had units in the area who could respond within two or three hours. If we didn't have units on standby on the anniversary of 9/11 with Benghazi being a hotspot for violence then that should be a concern. Our embassy is sovereign land of the United States and we have permission to protect our land anytime we damn well please, especially if our citizens are in jeopardy.

I wasn't in the White House and I don't know all the specifics. I know from news reports we supposedly had communication with the Central Intelligence Agency Annex Facility. I know we supposedly had drones in the area sending live feed back to the White House, so we could determine more clearly what was going on. I know we have to have plans in place for these sorts of things with troops ready to be deployed at a moment's notice. The message we sent to the world, to our citizens and to those left behind is one of impotence. We did nothing. It matters because that decision cost four Americans their lives.

It is easy for me to play Monday morning quarterback and cast blame around. We all do it, and we all do it really well. My gut just tells me this sends a loud message to our enemies that we are not going to act when we need to. It does not build trust with our people we have spread across the world that we have their back and it does not speak well of an Administration when they can't get their story right. Where was the President throughout the night while we were being attacked and our people killed? What was he doing to help our people? Who gave the stand down order and why? If it wasn't the President who gave the stand down order then doesn't that raise all type of new questions? It is just a big clusterfrig and people, OUR people, are dead. "Peace through Strength" means we not only have the means to act swiftly, but we do it when needed. It sends a message to all that the United States is not to be threatened. Sending in four helicopters and four fighter jets or any number of combinations with the goal of extracting our people was the right thing to do. Our military was probably demanding to go and not understanding why the "GO" order wasn't given. Displaying strength is essential and having a strong military is not enough. We have to act in moments like this to really be taken seriously. We don't do it to prove a point or to gain bragging rights. We make these decisions to get our people because it is the right thing to do. It is who we are as Americans.

If the United States had plenty of money, I would love to have 18 active aircraft carriers. Just imagine two aircraft carriers parked off the East Coast, two parked off the West Coast and two more on the other side of Cuba. The other twelve deployed around the world with others in dry-dock being upgraded. We need to invest heavily in expanding our elite Special Forces program. These forces are the ones that are most equipped to go after terrorist. The United States needs to have the most elite Special Forces and related nimble forces as well as the big, bulky military the world is used to seeing.   We have spending issues, so we need to be responsible with our military and still provide the upgrades needed to reign as the Super Power of the world. Again, "Peace through Strength" works. Countries need to know killing our citizens, ambassadors, or attacking us in any way is not tolerated and we will respond.

The other area of military expansion to develop is the Cyber Age response to weaken the infrastructure of attacking countries or cells. Developing the technology to wipe out power grids, infect computer technology and confuse target identification, so the enemy targets their own resources for destruction thinking it is our forces. These military advancements will result in saving American soldiers by reducing "boots on the ground" combat operations and continue sending the message to the world America is not to be provoked.

I know 400 – 600 billion is not enough to fund our military and it exposes us to risks. I also know we have to cut spending and it means cutting across the board. There are ways to still protect and defend America on a smaller budget. There are creative ways to examine cost and develop a strategy that does not compromise our military, our people or our nation. I don't have all the answers. I just hope I have a piece of the puzzle. There are great minds out there who can detail out a comprehensive plan to provide an incredible defense, plan for the future and do so within the recommended budget. Again, cuts have to happen and while the military is a necessity, it still needs to live within its means.

Debt Owed & Debt the US Owes

Another area of confusion is the debt owed to us by other countries. What is up with this? Countries expect us to pay back the money they loaned us, right? When and where did our elected officials start waiving countries from the obligation of paying us the debt owed us, the people of the United States? Did you know prior to Egypt running a "lapse" on our embassy protection Egypt was trying to get the United States to wave the debt they owed the American people (Greenhouse, 1991; Ritz,

2012)? This debt was in the billions. The
Obama Administration was considering
agreeing to wipe their debt clean. It may be
done anyway despite the disastrous 9/11
debacle this past year. In the words of John
McEnroe, "Surely, you can't be serious (Kass,
2012)."

Collect the DEBT owed to us by other
nations. Begin a repaying system to begin in
the year 2020. This money would go directly
towards paying off the national debt or back to
the American people. Let me say it another
way. No more absolving countries of their
responsibility to pay the United States back for
what they borrowed unless we get the same
treatment. End of story. This can and probably
has become a national security nightmare. If
we give them the money it is one thing.
Allowing them to borrow money is another.
Borrowing implies a form of enslavement.

As stated already, no borrowing of
money from other nations. The national

security risks of getting into to bed with another country financially are dangerous. It makes a country impotent and reduces the ability to project strength. At the end of the day, China and Japan hold some of our debt (Isidore, 2012). We can only be so bold with them. We need them. This smells of problems and corruption, not to mention, breeches in security related areas.

Immigration

Develop and pass legislation by 2015 that effectively deals with our immigration issue in our country. Examine how we can secure borders with the current forces and methods we have now. Don't increase spending or throw money at something hoping it sticks. Examine solutions. Governor Perry said in the presidential debates he could fix the border issues within 12 to 18 months if he were elected president (Hannity, 2011). Get together with those familiar with the problem and come up with something that is going to work. We are talking about people coming across the Mexican border primarily into our country without going through the appropriate, legal process. This can't be hard to figure out. Throwing money at the problem is not the solution. It may end up being part of the solution, but not the solution. Break it down and take it apart so a long term solution can be figured it out. While nothing is a 100% except death, there is a way to significantly slow illegal immigration into our country. Our national security is at risk here and if we can't fix something like this in our own country how in the hell do we think we can fix something in another country.

The amount of conversation and debate we have had as a nation over the years is pathetic. Talk is cheap. It is almost like we don't want to fix the problem. Again, we put a man on the Moon. This isn't even close. We have a spending problem, so we have to be careful to examine the solution and work within our means. We have to decide if America is going to enforce the laws on the books about illegal immigration and if so, enforce them; if not, change it to reflect what America is going to do consistently. No need to have laws that are not enforced. For those in the country illegally, consider a method to allow a "work visa" or "green card" status for those who are obeying our laws and demonstrating good in the community. This will rub some conservatives the wrong way, but America is not going to deport someone who is in good standing and the only law he or she broke was coming to the greatest country in the world to have a better life for himself /herself and their family (Moffett, 2012). Any conservative who challenges this, needs to reflect on their respective values.

We want people to come to this country and we hope and pray each comes the legal way. However, we don't begrudge anyone for trying any means to get the greatest country in the world. We are a nation of immigrants. We love immigrants. We love it when someone defects to our country. We want others to want to come here. We just have to figure out a way for them to do it that makes sense legally and doesn't put our nation at risk.

To summarize an effective strategy for reform:

- *Enforce laws on the books. Since that is not going to happen, do the following...*
- Secure the Borders. Build 25 foot fence along the southern border. Insure fences are either transparent or can be seen through by the American side of the fence. Insert National Guard stations every three to five miles. Patrol consistently. Establish clear rules for engagement. Once the law is clearly stated, those caught crossing are sent immediately back. There is no detaining, delay or loop hole to side step (confirm illegal is not a terrorist)

- Add Coast Guard ships, patrols and more personnel and run more patrols
- Those who are here illegally need to get in line behind those who are already in line and go through the process legally. Add additional immigration employees to speed up the process if needed. Issue work visa(s) or green card(s), so the individual can work in America and pay taxes on their income like everyone else.
- While the individual, who is in America illegally, is waiting in line to pursue citizenship, insure he or she has photo identification, finger printed for background checks and understands he or she needs to abide by all laws or he or she will be automatically deported. Also, make sure they learn to speak and understand English.
- Link everything back to social programming. Insure those who came to America illegally are either

unqualified for these safety net programs for seven years or until the individual becomes an American citizen (whichever is longer). And then do it.

- The individual entering illegally cannot vote until he or she becomes an American citizen (sounds silly I know, but voter fraud is a reality).

- Limit student visas. Round them up and send them home. There is no need for this program until there is way to track the students to insure compliance.

- Insure there is a system for tracking those who come to America, track their movements and insure they do not overstay their designated time period. They are visitors.

- Decide what the law is, put it in place and execute it consistently from a set point hence- forth. For example, if the goal is to have all those go through the process legally and the border secure by

2015, then make it clear to all; beginning in 2015, any illegal entries to the United States results in "this" consequence. If it is deportation then deport.

- Once new laws are in place, enforce the law without discrimination. The message needs to be very simple. If you seek to come to America there is a proper way to come through our borders. Come here legally. If you come illegally, then we will deport you. It really needs to be simple, but simple involves deportation immediately if the law is not honored. State what the law is, enforce the law and be consistent with the process. No "ifs" or "buts." After a certain date, illegal immigrants are deported. This also means for those who are already here, but refuse to come out of the shadows and register. The law has to have teeth that are immediate for those who did not come to America through the proper channels. Any ambiguity or loop holes in the law will exasperate the already colossal problem facing us today.

Will this keep out people from crossing our borders? No. Will people find a way to enter into the greatest country in the world illegally? Yes. I am not crazy about building a fence and having a massive border patrol. To me, it does not reflect liberty. It sounds like the wall dividing East and West Germany prior to its collapse in the late 1980s. Maybe there are other ways to secure the border that haven't been considered. To me, the key is the law. If you obey the law and follow the process then there is a place for you in our country, provided you want to embrace America and live by our standards. If you break the law by your entry into our country, then we send you back from where you came and encourage you to follow the process America has in place. It must be immediate and consistent.

      While a lot of people, conservatives and liberals, have in their plan to hit businesses hard for hiring illegal immigrants, I don't agree with this process. I don't think businesses in America need to control illegal immigration. Business owners can complete the necessary background checks and related forms associated with legal status. But hitting businesses with a hefty fine by the government for hiring illegal immigrants seems to be an over-step on the government's part in regards to liberty.

      Another issue many don't discuss is individuals coming to America to have their babies. This is not a southern border issue only. There are many who fly in to America from all over the world to have their babies here. In a lot of cases, they fly out after delivery after the mother is cleared for travel. This is a big issue because the baby born on American soil is a citizen. Let's say the family flies in for the sole purpose of having their baby be an American citizen. Assume the couple is from a country that does not embrace American values. If I am correct, and I may be wrong, then the baby born on American soil is considered a natural born citizen. Even though he or she may not live here and may grow up in an environment that spits in the face of everything America stands for, he or she is still an American citizen. Can that individual be elected President of the United States? Immigration reform needs to address this issue. No one need be allowed into our country for the purpose of having their child be born on American soil and then going back to their home country. I think this is a huge national security issue. While there may not be a way to prevent this from happening entirely, there needs to be steps in place that prevent entry of a female or couple who are already pregnant to America until after her child is born in her home country.

Middle East

The Middle East is simpler than most people believe. Most make it complex, but there is no secret to the issue. The Palestrians and the Israelis will not hammer out a peace treaty embraced by all those involved. It is not going to happen. The United States needs to cease and desist. While America will not stop the bloodshed that has existed for years, we can continue to offer a solution that may help all parties. The first part is we are allies with Israel and there is no dispute about our loyalty and friendship. We will continue to provided 20+ billion in aid to Israel annually and embrace our Friend for the world to see.

The message to the Arab nations and those seeking to build a Palestinian nation is simple. The United States will provide you financial incentive to live in peace with Israel. America will also invest time in imploring other nations to stand up against the anti-sematic intent of those countries seeking to destroy

Israel. It is the role of the Arab communities to encourage their people to embrace this reality or to suffer the consequences. The United States will up their monthly aide to the Arab people. The money we send will be significant and only have four expectations:

- Live at peace with Israel by not being involved in, or approving of, any attacks of any kind on Israelis or their country
- No development of nuclear energy or bombs or weapons of mass destruction
- No training, supporting or involvement with terrorists of any kind
- No attacks on Americans or what we deem is America (embassy, ships, etc)

The consequence for breaking any of the above results in missing monthly payments until the Arab community fixes the problem – however long it takes. The money will not restart until the problem is dealt with in a satisfactory manner from the US and Israeli perspective. It is clear and without malice towards any country and leaves zero grounds for misinterpretation. The key will be for American leaders to be consistent and steadfast. If the Arab community does not want our money then this agreement won't matter. If the funding helps with their way of life and they can live in harmony with Israel then mission accomplished.

Our current approach smells of inconsistency and cannot be taken seriously. The cycle is predictable and is insane. The definition of insanity is often referred to as "doing the same thing over and over hoping for different results." We see this all the time in the weight loss industry. Eating well, watching caloric intake, and exercising are the key to weight loss. Even more simply stated, "Eat less...Do more." Still, people buy magazines, videos, join gyms, join weight loss programs, and try the latest diet regiment. Most quit after a short time with little lasting benefit. We have all been there. As pathetic of an example as the above just was it is where America is with the Middle East.

It needs to be simple. If we can help the Arab community financially and the Arab community wants our money, the tax payer's money, than we are glad to help, provided, the Arab leader(s) are willing to comply with the expectations. It is always good to build relationships and attempt to forge a bond with all the leaders in every country. We don't need a lot of dialogue if that is a problem. What America wants is results. What America expects are no sanctioned, approved, unapproved attacks on Israel. Israel will not attack unless attacked. We know Israel will not attack unless threatened. The world knows this as demonstrated by their constant restraint as Israelis are constantly threatened, attacked and plotted against by those considering Israel an illegitimate country. If for some reason Israel does attack, then America supports Israel.

Short, neat and simple.

We can't impose democracy on the Middle East. Either they are not ready for it or they just don't want it. There are too many sects disagreeing with one another over there and their culture does not allow for freedom. It's for them to choose and their right to live in the way they want to live. We do not need to muddy the waters by trying to rescue their people when the whole do not want to be rescued.

Using another poor example, Life Guards (Brouhard, 2011) are taught repeatedly how to save someone who is drowning. In almost all the training, they are instructed to offer the drowning person a buoy or floating device and guide the person to safety. The reason for this is to protect the Life Guard. Drowning people usually panic because they are fighting for their life and focused on survival. Drowning people seldom listen to reason or see the big picture. They tend to fight with the Life

189

Guard, who is trying to help them. There have been cases where both the drowning person and Life Guard drown because the Life Guard cannot control the person.

Keeping good boundaries and positioning ourselves appropriately is essential to a successful Middle East strategy. We want them to want democracy and freedom. We can't make them receive it. There are too many players involved and too many unknowns that never break well for the United States. We need to put the responsibility for change and conformity on the leadership of the Middle East community. Israel isn't going anywhere and neither are they. Israel is not going to give back land and the Islamic communities aren't going to take it back. Israel is not going to allow Palestinians to hold elective office in Israel and Israel is going to be distrustful of the Arab community at large. These things are not going to change and the United States playing the peace tape over and over as if it matters now more than yesterday is absurd. Our Intelligence Officers will continue to gather information and develop Assets. We will continue to know everything we can about those in power, those wanting power and the people who are caught in the middle. But to quote an old saying, "Money talks and BS walks." The United States needs to say what we mean and mean what we say. Back it up in deed. Keep it simple.

Military Bases

In regards to our military bases around the world, it is impressive if you look up in how many countries we have personnel in around the world. It is easy to see why Congressman Ron Paul (Paul, 2011) calls this excessive spending and why other countries may perceive this as being bullish on our part. In this day and age, I don't think we can really afford to close all our bases or embassies. I would like to personally. I would like to say to countries, "Fine, you don't like us or want us in your country, we will leave." We pull out and kick them to the curb. No problems here. However, that is not who America is and engaging in this behavior puts America at risk.

In 1974, Francis Ford Coppola conducted a sequel to *The Godfather*. Michael Carleone, played brilliantly by Al Pacino, said, "Keep your friends close and your enemies closer" (Lewis, 2011). This statement is very appropriate for the United States when implementing a national defense strategy (although Israel may not think the strategy may be good for them). You want to know what your opposition is doing and being in their neighborhood is essential to getting good information. The number of bases around the world we have is a quiet reminder to the world that the United States can be anywhere we need to be faster than any other country in the world. Don't think other countries are not completely aware of this fact. While we may be able to cut some costs and look at the budget more closely to determine excess spending, Peace through Strength works.

Home Land Security

I was not a big fan of creating yet another department in our government. Even with the reality of the 9/11 attack, I still think it is an over extension of government to develop a department that insures that all branches communicate with one another. To me, it is absurd to think this is going to do anything but create more confusion. Our national defense needs only the Department of Defense (DOD), Federal Bureau of Investigation (FBI) and the Central Intelligence Agency (CIA). Throwing more money at more government is not the answer. If there are problems, fix the problems with the three agencies mentioned above. The less cooks you have in the kitchen the better. It is amazing how adding more people, more programs to the mix, does not fix problems. It adds to the chaos. Perfecting the basics will go a long way to keeping America safe. I know we haven't had an attack since Fort Hood (which is referred to as workplace violence), but creating more bureaucracy is never the answer. Insure the DOD, FBI and CIA are communicating with each other. The FBI is the one who needs to communicate with local law enforcement. There is a way to make this easy and productive that safeguards Americans. Closing the loop by increasing cooperation and communication at all levels has to do with good solid relationship building.

Space

"Space; The final frontier... To boldly go where no man has gone before" (Day, 2005). This was the opening line off Star Trek, which aired in the 1960s. The United States landed on the Moon in 1969 (Moskowitz, 2012). Space is the ultimate area to conquer and given its limitlessness it appears we are on the beginning stages of discovery. I don't know if we need to have a base on the Moon. I am sure it cost a lot of money and involves a lot of unpredictable elements. However, we cannot allow another country to beat us at building a base there. So, with that in mind, there is a need to have a base on the Moon. There is a need for the United States to control and dominate the world of space. The following is such a vague plan that it doesn't warrant mention. One might say that about this whole book. Like everything else I mentioned in this book, I have no background in this area. I certainly cannot speak about Space or anything related to it with any integrity. I just know that the United States of America needs to lead the way in this area as it will become extremely valuable in the next 200 years.

We need to build a base on the Moon by 2028. We need to use the Moon to launch a visit to Mars and plan to land on Mars by 2038. If this is successful and America sees an opportunity then we need to build a base on Mars by 2050. We can't do this without dealing with our spending and debt first. In no way am I advocating spending more money than we have allocated until we get our budget under control. The economy is first and foremost. What I am saying is it is important to dominate space and we can't take this for granted. Having a base on the Moon is symbolic and communicates to the rest of the world America is the greatest nation on earth and, until we find out otherwise, we are the greatest in the galaxy.

Chapter 7
Constitutional
Amendment(s)

"There are two ways to conquer and enslave a country. One is by the sword. The other is by debt"

John Adams

Balance Budget

A balance budget amendment for the federal government is important and our current financial house illustrates why this is so. The United States of America is not required to balance its budget and live within its means. How can anything exist in this day and age without a budget? We just spend and spend and spend, while kicking the can down the road regarding cuts we need to make, in hopes it just goes away. In therapy, we would call that denial. A good therapist would help the individual confront the denial in their life and see how he or she was going to deal with it. We see how elected officials have dealt with it and it is not encouraging. We need to put some accountability in the Constitution regarding this matter to insure that this lackadaisical approach does not infect future generations.

The amendment needs to define what a balance budget is and what the consequence or timeline is should the federal government not balance the budget by the end of each fiscal year. War or unforeseen disasters may qualify as causes to borrow money or not meet budget. This needs to be clarified, so it doesn't serve as a loophole for any endeavor to be deemed a disaster. The bottom line is our founders never dreamt of a day when we would borrow and borrow and engage in the irresponsible behavior we have for the last one hundred years.

President Barack Obama called President George W. Bush irresponsible and unpatriotic for accumulating almost six trillion in debt in eight years (Doherty, 2012). I was not in Bush's shoes and did not have the pressure he had of keeping America safe after 9/11. I don't necessarily fault him for his decision making. However, hindsight is often 20/20. Paying down the debt and focusing on the economy, while protecting America, would have been my three pronged approach knowing what I know now. Instead, we got spread out and possibly lost sight of the intent of the attacks. The attacks weren't just to kill Americans. The attacks were on our way of life and our financial standing in the world. The Twin Towers, in the heart of New York, were targeted as much for what they represented to the world as anything else.

President Obama was wrong for engaging in even worse spending behavior by increasing the debt six more trillion in only four years (Jeffrey, 2012). Even the great President, Ronald Regan, increased the national debt (Blodget, 2012) as have other presidents throughout our history. Enough is enough and it will only stop when there is a constitutional requirement imposing the responsibility upon the politicians to govern responsibly. Low to zero debt; continued strong economic growth and protecting our country and its people are the three layers of what the federal government needs to be about. There is of course more to it than the three, but these three are the big three.

For the last four years the federal government has run virtually without a budget in place. President Obama submitted a budget to the Senate for the last two years, but in both cases, they vetoed it 100% without President Obama receiving one Democrat votes (Jaffe, 2011). The Democrat Party controlled the Senate and still they refused to sign on to it because of the ramifications it would mean for them going into a voting year. The budget called for spending to increase to over one trillion of the total revenue slated to come in to the federal government. The House passed a budget the last two years and it was sent to the Senate, but the Senate would never call it to the Floor to be voted on because of what it contained. Instead of something happening, nothing happened because apparently, the government doesn't need a budget. This whole process is an example of why we, as a country, are in debt up to our eyeballs.

Cap Borrowing

Cap borrowing and total debt accumulation to no more than 35% of GDP. Tie this into the amendment listed above or in some way to show how these are compatible. For example, the United States may have to go to war and the annual budget did not allow for this emergent need. There has to be a way to pay for it and the budget has to allow for this provision while offering sound fiscal decision making. Again, the loop holes are to be closed and there has to be minimal wiggle room for elected officials to alter the meaning and intent of this amendment.

Someone once asked me, "Who do we really owe this money to and what happens if we just refuse to pay anymore. Are these countries really going to go to war with us?" I think my friend has a point. Most of our debt is borrowed from us. We could reset the clock and just erase it and start over. Tom Clancy wrote a great book called *Debt of Honor*. It involved a country trying to wreck our financial institutions and the American currency. In the end, America just reset the clock and started over. We could refuse to pay our debt back and dare countries to come and get it. While countries may not go to war with us, this irresponsible behavior of not paying back our debt would sink our currency and impact the global economy for a zillion years. My guess is we have to pay our debt down and we have to stop increasing the money borrowed. The bleeding has to stop and it has to stop now.

Chapter 8
Trial by Jury

"We must reject the idea that every time a law's broken, society is guilty rather than the lawbreaker. It is time to restore the American precept that each individual is accountable for his actions"

Ronald Reagan, 1968

Conservative Messaging

In the United States, we are tried in a court of law by our peers. A twelve person jury is selected for trial by jury and a judge serves as the expert on the law. Evidence is submitted to the jury to evaluate; after all the information is considered a jury renders a verdict. The future of the Republican Party remains undetermined and America will judge whether capitalism has any relevancy or not based on the next four years. Republicans need to stand up for conservative principles and for them to do so they themselves must understand these principles. What I mean is continually relate and connect everything back to financial responsibility. Be the grown-ups in the room and before the media. Don't be difficult against making deals as long as each deal includes significant references to *Cut, Cap, Reform and Balance.* Accountability is a soft term people may use when referring to politics or business. In this situation, I prefer the word "trial" because the American people will have a real decision to make in the next four years.

You might wonder why the Democrat Party is not on trial. The Democrat Party is shielded in many ways by the Press (Noyes, 2012)) and the lack of true journalistic coverage exposing their agenda. This is mainly because the Press identifies with liberalism and wants this ideology to spread across America. The Press will put the blame at every turn on the Republicans, which is why the Republicans have to be the ones who are on the offensive. In the past, Democrats have been proactive about attacking the Republican agenda and twisting it into something it is not. Republicans react rather than respond and they end up looking like elitist idiots. The tables need to be proactively turned and a strategy to assault and malign the Democrat agenda needs to be launched. The key is for the Republicans to communicate every way possible with the American people on the Republican rationale, but making it into a positive rather than a negative. They also need to directly attack and expose the Democrat agenda.

John Boehner, who is the Speaker of the House, and all his Republican colleagues should have a unified message whenever speaking with the Press or the Public. While Congressman Boehner may be the Speaker of the House, he is not the best at delivering a message. This objective may need to be accomplished by someone else who is charismatic and well spoken. Think about how Senate Majority Leader Harry Reid comes across on television. He is not the hope of the Democrat Party – Barack is. Who is the next leader of the Republican Party? Who is it that can present conservatism in a way, without notes, that conveys to the American people who we are as a country? This is the team of persons who need to lead this charge. All others need to share in it and be unified, but people follow those who move them. Think Reagan.

The message needs to echo change-talk and positive expression. The message needs to be heard in this way. "Americans voted in 2012 to reelect President Obama for a second term. The majority of the people believe his path to prosperity for the American people is the best approach. The same America reelected the Republicans majority in the House to continue to balance out the spending habits of the Democrats. The Republican Party disagrees with continuing to spend in the reckless manner currently being done by the Democrats. Republicans strongly believe in conservatism.

We believe in the individual and her ability to make her own decisions, chart her own course and accomplish her own dreams. We believe in capitalism and small business growth that only thrives under less bureaucracy and less government interference. We believe in America being energy independent by the development of oil, coal, fracking, natural gas as well as pursuing alternative sources of energy.

We believe pursing energy independence will have a watershed effect on job growth in America and at the same time, drive the cost of gasoline and energy down for American citizens. While we disagree with the President's approach and policies, we want to honor those who want to see the President be successful. Republicans are agreeable to work with the Democrats to insure America gets back on her feet.

To do this in a responsible way, proposals have to include, *cuts* to federal spending, a *cap* to federal spending, *reforms* to entitlements and a goal towards a *balanced* budget. Democrats can move forward with their plans they believe make America great and as long as it does not involve irresponsible financial decisions we will consider their plan. They believe they have the answers to make America's economy strong again and to put more people to work in the private sector. The Democrat plan will involve more federal spending, zero cuts or reform to entitlements and social programming, more regulation on businesses and more debt. The people will need to judge over the next four years if they are better off due to the liberal policies of Democrats or do the people see the need for a return to the capitalistic and conservative principles that made America, America and the world's greatest super power?"

If the Republicans hit this message in every instance throughout the next four years and market this comparison at all times in all ways then the people may hear it and the Press may be forced to at least address it with some level of accountability. The Republicans can't go off script and have mixed messages out there. It has to be united if indeed the Party believes this is the right course. They can't have a bunch of "eggheads" out there representing Republican principles. I am not advocating that elected officials be robots or Party followers and drink the Kool-Aid. What I am saying is

Democrats find the five or eight nut-jobs out there who are on the Republican ticket somewhere and link each to representing conservatism. Republicans have to do better and be prepared to have answers prior to the crisis, rather than always reacting and defending. Republicans and conservatives (not always the same) need to respond rather than react to adverse questions and situations. *They need to teach conservatism and capitalism.*

The Democrats are planning to put their failures on Republicans because they can count on the Republicans to fight them at every turn. Liberals are not about success, but about power. If liberals can wipe out the political opposition then liberals can advance their agenda of creating a social nanny-state in America. It has everything to do with power and staying in power and as long as the Republicans continue to do the lifting for the Democrats in regards to taking the fall the game will not change. Standing up and telling the American people what the Republicans are going to do, why they are going to do it and asking the people to evaluate the success of liberalism is the only way to expose the problem of liberalism. Republicans can't be stubborn or difficult. They just need to pass their ideas and dare the Senate and the President to send them something reflecting real change. Too much attention is on what the Republican are to do. The focus needs to be what are Democrats to do? Pass Legislation and communicate with the people.

Republican Identity Crisis

Before Republicans can be effective they have to figure out what does a Republican stand for in 2013 and beyond. I don't think they know. Republicans are so divided and there is even talk of starting a 3rd party (Democrats would love for the conservative base to split into another party). Ronald Reagan referenced not having a third Party, but actually having a second Party. The identity of the Republican

Party has long been at odds with itself. Are they conservative or not? What brand of conservatism are they and how does that even make sense? Do they have the stomach for sticking to conservative principles? If the liberals continue to be successful with smearing and blaming Republicans and the Republicans remain reactive and defensive then an opportunity to teach and promote the ideals that made America great is lost.

The Republicans appear to want to water down their values and beliefs in conservative principles to be competitive with Democrats, rather than playing hard-ball and exposing the problem with liberalism. The problem is government wanting power and control, not individuals wanting freedom. Individual liberties, opportunity, pursuit of happiness, achieving the "American Dream," and being free from government rule make up conservatism. Sadly, the Republican Party gets side-tracked on other issues and it confuses the

American people on where the Party stands. The Party doesn't want to offend, they come off as wanting to please and the media pounces on these defects because they are defects. It is going on right now as the Right is trying to digest how to combat the loss of Governor Romney. What more can the Republicans capitulate?

Republicans have always been for the individual. Somehow Republicans have been reduced to being just for the rich (who are individuals) and that paradigm has been reinforced to the American people over the last 40 to 50 years. Republicans supposedly want less government. Republicans supposedly want individuals to make their own decisions. Republicans supposedly want the Constitution to be followed and honored in America. There is nothing wrong with these principles. So why do Republicans behave as if there is something to be ashamed of?

The Republican Party has an opportunity over the next twelve years to really solidify itself as the Party for the majority of the American people. The American people are as involved in politics now as ever before. The difference between the 2008 Presidential election and the 2012 Presidential election is performance. People wanted change in 2008 and they got caught up in the mystic and charisma of then Senator Barack Obama. His performance in Office was effective enough to be reelected. Although the President was reelected, I would argue the conservative base did not show up for Governor Romney. The Governor received a good portion of Independent votes, but the Minority vote went whole-heartedly to President Obama. The vote most people don't discuss is the number of conservatives who did not vote for the President or the Governor. They sent a message and the Republicans need to listen.

The Republicans have to get their house in order and figure out what they stand for and how to market it throughout the country. People are interested like never before. Arguments can be made about a changing American culture and the number of people on the government dole. These are issues to bring up and discuss, but what does the Republicans want the public to focus on over the next four years? What do they want the people to hear? Mapping out a strategy to sell America on conservatism and then actually practicing it is the key for a successful Republican ground campaign. The key is what do Americans pay attention to through the eyes of the media? Do they focus on the Republicans being difficult in the House and holding "Hope and Change" up? Do they see the full cooperation of the Republican Party working for the good of the American People for what they voted for in 2012, while the Republicans *positively* disclaim to the world their fundamental disagreement

with the effectiveness of the liberal agenda?
Teach America conservatism. Teach capitalism.
Teach about the Constitution.

Americans across the country can
connect the dots. The problem with the
Republican strategy in the 2012 presidential
campaign was Romney under estimated the
hold the media has over the American people
through the air-waves. The message was good,
but it did not filter through to the uninformed.
The Republicans need to use the next four years
to tell the story of conservatism and how it
brings hope and freedom to individuals and
reacquaint the American people with their
American heritage. They also need to set up
camp in those tightly contested districts in
Ohio, Virginia, and Florida. While the
Republicans engage in this strategy they also
need to allow liberalism to be revealed and
constantly ask the people which they prefer,
which is more American?

People understand the concept of giving someone enough rope to either hang him or herself or to have enough slack to work on untying the knot so he or she can be free. The Republicans need to hold the line on financial issues and allow Democrats to attempt to side-track Americans with their focus on social issues. Again, the Republicans will get the blame if there is blame needed. The key is to change the narrative to the American people and the way to do that is to allow liberalism to be released on the wallet of the American People.

Some people have to experience the hot plate of the stove is hot before they learn not to touch it. The Republicans keep trying to protect America by pushing their hand away from the hot plate of the stove. This isn't working. Let the people touch the hot plate and see if they like the heat or not. In this case, it is the so-called "Fiscal Cliff." Republicans need to make no deals unless it deals with the core issues of

Cut, Cap, Reform and Balance. It needs to be significant. Remember, at the Democrat Convention and during the course of the campaign the Democrats cited the tax policies under Clinton as being representative of economic growth.

In the end, it comes down to money. Most Americans, despite political parties, agree with fiscal responsibility. The problem Republicans have is they don't always demonstrate conservative principles. They come across almost schizophrenic in their decision making. On one hand the Republicans cry out about the deficit, debt and spending. On the other hand, they have racked up debt, done little with the deficit and have spent their share of the tax payers hard earned dollars. If Republicans demonstrated conservative principles the majority of Americans of all races and gender will follow them. The Republicans would have such a large lead among Democrats that the hard-core liberals would not be able to hold America hostage like it has the last four years. So how do Republicans get there? We have already discussed key strategies in the above pages, but below are some more related topics Republicans need to consider if they are to carry their message to the individual.   In my opinion, there are about forty percent Republicans and forty percent Democrats that vote along party lines. I think the Republican Party could sway four percent of the Democrat forty percent to vote Republican.   I think Republicans can get a majority of Independent voters as well. If Republicans actually taught and lived conservatism, capitalism and promoted individual liberty Republicans would carry 55% or more in every presidential election.

Fiscal Responsibility

Take a look at spending. President Ronald Reagan created one of the biggest economic recoveries the United States has ever known. After taking Office in 1981 and having a slow year, with the nation on the decline, the revered President, Ronald Wilson Reagan, and his policies assisted in 40+ months of job growth (Sperry, 2001 & Ferrara, 2011). Through his lowering of taxes and deregulation, Reagan grew sixteen million jobs during the course of his presidency. The problem associated with Reagan from a Democrat perspective is he never balanced the annual budget and he increased the national debt. There are other arguments too, but these two stick out when Republicans stick their chests out and lecture about spending issues.

President Jimmy Carter, who is considered by conservatives as one of the worst presidents ever, created 10 million jobs in four years. Ronald Reagan beat President Carter by a landslide in the 1980 presidential race. The people were dissatisfied with Carter. The Iran hostage debacle went on for 444 days, the economy was poor and the mood of the country was thirsting for change. However, 10 million jobs are 10 million jobs. Not sure where they all came from or what the break down is, but it is still a lot of jobs in a four year stretch. Reagan did not create 10 million jobs in his first term in office.

President George H. Bush was one of the most qualified politicians we have ever had in the White House. He was in the military, fought in World War II and was shot down as a fighter pilot. He was an Ambassador, served as Director of the Central Intelligence Agency, served as Vice President for eight years, where he learned firsthand how to grow the economy and stimulate job growth. What did that get him? He said, "Read my lips. No new taxes." What did he do? He raised taxes (Norquist, 2011). Well, if the trick to raising revenue for the federal government is cutting taxes why in the world would he go back on his word and raise taxes. It was political suicide. Not to mention Mr. Ross Perot running as a third party candidate. Ultimately the votes cast to

Mr. Perot were taken from Mr. Bush and that helped soon to be President Clinton become 42nd President of the United States.

President Clinton actually balanced the budget, did not add to the national debt as much, created 22 million jobs and left approximately a 500 billion dollar surplus (Davis, 2012) for President George W. Bush. Republicans cringe over this fact and then cite he was helped by the Republicans Congress who held his feet to the fire. Maybe that was true, but he gets the credit in the eyes of Americans. The bottom line is Republicans have blown it over the years at cutting spending and getting America's financial house in order and all the blustering can't change this long-held perspective.

If Republicans want to have creditability beyond the rank and file then they have to be good stewards of the tax payer's money. Their mantra is *Cut, Cap, Reform and Balance*. Republicans standing their ground in 2013 will result in continued low approval ratings for Congress and lead to a stand-off with the media. Accept and deal with it. Since the media is biased in favor of liberals, who do you think will try to frame the narrative for the people? More than likely, what will happen is the Republicans will give-in to the Democrats over the "Fiscal Cliff" (which they did) just as they did in April of 2010 when the Republicans were not going to risk the military go without pay. The Democrats cried out Republicans didn't care and the Republicans were accusing Democrats of holding the military hostage. Republicans blinked.

It won't be long before the Democrats claim the Republicans are holding the Middle Class hostage in allowing the Bush Tax Cuts to expire (which they did). So will the Republicans give in by kicking the can down the road for six months or so? The problem is the media shows the American people Republicans are the problem, rather than allowing liberalism to be evaluated. The strategy has to change for the Republican Party. They are now the minority in the eyes of media. The rules have changed. Republicans have to be aggressive, assertive, and continually pitching their message to the people through the media. For example, Senator Marco Rubio needs to be a weekly figure on CNN's top rated news show. Congressman Paul Ryan may need to secure a weekly spot on CBS's top rated news show. Senator Rand Paul may need to secure a weekly spot on NBC's top rated news show. Line up about thirty who can articulate the passion of being a conservative and how this helps the individual and have them on show after show, so conservatives are the ones dominating the airwaves, rather than the Democrats. It is great to speak on the FOX network, but real conservatives need to go where there aren't any. The key is to have people who, inspire and depict leadership; rather than some dull, old fart, who appears less exciting than watching paint dry.

Women Rights

The Republican Party does not have to broaden its base. Republicans have to clarify their message. As I said, Republicans have an identity disorder and it confuses the American people. Republicans are divided and unsure of what it means to be Republicans. America is divided and unsure what Republicans represent. Clarify and unite around conservative principles and the people will listen. The majority of Americans are conservatives in most of the way they think. However, what the Democrats do well is separate people into groups and cast fear into these groups, so they support Democrats rather than Republicans. Once the fear is in place then they offer something to ease that fear.

Take women. The famous "War on Women" slogan circulating during the 2012 presidential campaign (Arrillaga, 2012) was clever on the part of the Democrats. I kept hearing it all the time and yet, I couldn't think of one thing it represented that was based on truth. The media and Democrats had a field day with the response they were getting from Ms. Sandra Fluke testifying to Congress about the need for women to have access to free contraceptives.

I remember Jay Leno, who is a host of the Tonight Show on NBC, interviewing Dennis Miller, (Leno, 2012) who is a noted conservative. The two appeared to be friends or at least on a friendly basis. Mr. Leno turned to Mr. Miller and said something about "So this war on women…" Mr. Miller just rolled his eyes and turned to the Host and said, "What are you talking about?" There is more to women's issues than reproductive rights, but a lot of emphasis is placed on contraceptives and abortions. First, most women don't want free contraceptives. It is insulting to women for others to pay for their contraceptives. It is equally insulting to believe that women think men in the Republican Party want to end their Rights and send women back to the days before they had Rights. Women don't believe that, but if you listen to the mantra from the Left it is what they would have you to believe.

Since the Supreme Court rule in Roe v/s Wade, America has remained divided on the topic of abortion. Contrary to beliefs, no sane, rational individual wants babies aborted. No one wants to kill babies. The question is not if you are for or against abortion? The question is where does choice come into play for women? Women have fought long and hard for their Rights and while they are not where they want to be, there is no way in hell that they are going to return to days of old.

Historically, women have been viewed as property. Arranged marriages are one of the more mild indecencies to attack the liberties of women. While slavery and the treatment of Blacks were beyond words and remains a despicable, inerasable travesty in our nation's history, women did not earn the right to vote until the 1920 (Lewis, 2011). Blacks who were treated like animals and degraded in public by Whites for a century more were granted the right to vote before women. Women Rights groups are terrified of returning to days when they have less voice and the hard core conservatives represent this fear to women.

Life begins at conception is a spiritual belief. Some truly believe this, as I do, and others disagree. Science can offer up facts to support this claim and other scientists or medical professionals can counter this with why it is not the case. Abortion is not about killing babies for women. It is about their right to choose what to do with their body. From their perspective, they fought hard for their rights and anything seemingly infringing upon their rights is met with voting Democrat.

From a constitutional point of view, the woman has every right to make decisions concerning her body as it relates to a medical procedure. Government telling an individual what to do with his or her body is inconsistent with the Constitution. Here is the problem. A medical procedure option is different than carrying a life inside one's body. Whether one defines life as beginning at conception or further down the road is an argument / discussion for the American people to engage in. At some point, the little "bean" growing inside the belly of the woman becomes a living being. Once this is established, this baby is a soon to be citizen of the United States of America. America is all about protecting the rights of the innocent and those who can't defend themselves. The baby in the womb has Rights. It has nothing to do with women not having Rights, but for conservatives, it's about the defenseless baby who wants to live, but can't fight for him or herself. Republicans need to remain proactive in their approach to oppose abortion unless the woman's health is at risk, the woman has experienced rape or incest.

They need to stick to their principles. Women get this and for most, it is not a defining issue. There is a reason Democrats want to make it the "defining" issue and cast abortion as the only issue women care about.

What is a defining issue for Women is the path to make money and care for their family. Women want the economy to be straightened out. I think this is actually the number one issue facing women and most women would agree. Women want good paying jobs, opportunity and a secure nation as much, if not more than men. Women want the economy to work well and women are proud to be American and to live in the greatest nation on earth. Most women I know don't want someone else paying for their contraceptives. They want to own that responsibility and see that as yet another way to show the world they can care for their own needs. Women want to insure their rights as individuals are not in jeopardy with the conservative base.

Most women are fiscally conservative and understand they need to live within their means. There are a lot of women business owners who want decrease tax rates and less government red tape, so they can do business, make money and hire people. They understand the government needs to deal with entitlements and live within its means. Women understand the need for the military and having a strong national defense in order to project peace through strength. They get it. They just don't want to be yanked around by a bunch of men who think they know better for them on how women need to live their lives. Convince women Republicans are for the individual woman, while creating jobs and women will vote for the Conservative.

Again, conservative principles are largely embraced by the majority of Americans in their personal life. When it comes to equal pay, individuals don't want the same pay as everyone else in their place of employment.

Parents would be furious if their child, who earned As, was given Cs, so those who earned Fs could experience what it is like to have Cs in school. Olympic athletes would not show up if the Olympic Committee announced that there were not going to be anymore losers and all would be awarded medals because we are all winners at heart. All this inclusiveness is a load of crap and individuals know this and don't practice it in their own life. Competition is healthy. Women don't want to earn more than men because they are women. They want to earn more than men, earn more than the next woman and so on, because they are great at their job and kick the competition's butt.

Immigration & Minorities

Immigration was discussed earlier and while reform seems unlikely, the Republican Party could really add more creditability to immigrants if they can land serious immigration reform that works for all those involved. No one can please all the people involved, but if a general consensus can be made that makes sense and reflects the intent of the laws surrounding how to enter this country legally, then more minorities with immigration concerns will vote for Republicans. Again, Republicans are for individual rights and not the government telling individuals how to live. While regulation is embraced, it needs to promote the individual rather than add power to the government. It is the same way with immigration reform and if the Republicans can get close to something resembling respect for those in our country who want to be here, but did not come legally, then when they become citizens, they will, because of their work ethic and character, embrace conservative principles.

African Americans have long voted for Democrats and the Democrats have played to the Blacks in our country using fear. I don't mean all Democrats, but the Liberal base. It is easy to forget sometimes that President Lincoln was a Republican and that the 13, 14 and 15th Amendments in the Constitution demolishing slavery were due to the Republicans (The National Black Republican Association). When Eugene "Bull" Connor in Alabama turned the water hoses and dogs on Dr. Martin Luther King, a Republican, as his followers walked through Birmingham, Alabama, in a peaceful protest of segregation and bigotry, we need to remember that Bull Connor was a Democrat. When the Civil Rights legislation of 1964 was up for a vote, it was the Republicans who voted it into legislation. There was more opposition from Democrats than from Republicans. Yes, Republicans have had their share of racists in their ranks, but so have the Democrats.

All throughout history there have been individuals who verbalized hideous remarks about African Americans. There are other minorities who have been demonized as well. Political parties have changed as well over time in various ways. The problem is somehow the

Republican Party allowed conservatism to be associated as the party for the wealthy and those who discriminate against others. This is the Republicans fault. Republicans being defined and classified by the media and Democrats is expected, but where is the fight to set the record right.

The message of individual opportunity appeals to African Americans in our country and it is why we are seeing an increase of African Americans come out for conservative ideas. It is interesting to note that when Blacks come out for conservatism there are a lot of racist comments thrown out towards them for "selling out (Wright, 2012)." However, when Black conservatives accuse Black liberals of "staying on the government plantation" (O'Reilly & Bishop Jackson, 2012), there are cries for apologies and marches. There is division among Blacks on just how successful the Democrat Party has truly been in helping their plight. When one looks at the numbers and see how many Blacks are still in poverty, how many children are in single parent homes, Black-on-Black crime and the educational advancements that have had lack luster results for their communities, it is hard to see significant progress?

African Americans are increasingly frustrated with the hate speech and the accusatory manner in which they have been represented. They are seeking to embrace principles reflecting conservative values and are open-minded to the possibilities existing in ideology reform. They know the current policies of the last forty years are not working for them and may be willing to give Republicans a try if Republicans can get their house in order.

Minorities are tired of being jerked around too. The level of abuse and violence imposed upon them throughout our history is brutal. Republicans need to remind minorities that they, Republicans, are the Party who was largely formed to oppose slavery in 1854. They need to remind Latinos that they champion small business and want them to live, here, in the greatest country in the world. We are all immigrants in one way or another. They need to remind Latinos that President Obama had all branches of government his first two years and could have passed immigration reform, but did not. At least President George W. Bush attempted to pass immigration legislation. The Republicans need to actively convey to all Minorities they are for the individual and that under their leadership the individual is allowed to be who, he or she wants to be and the only limits placed on their achievements are what is self-imposed. If Republicans do this and live it then Liberalism will crumble like the Iron Curtain.

Republican Leadership

The Republican leadership needs to hold monthly / quarterly press conferences that are tailored towards the individual at home watching television, rather than talking points and media question / answer time. They need to hold a board meeting with the American people and discuss progress towards *Cut, Cap, Reform and Balance* each month/quarter, teach conservatism and capitalism, and where they, Republicans, are headed during the course of that budget year. They need to conduct themselves with the American people in a way showing accountability and allow the people to evaluate their progress in a fair way throughout, rather than waiting until election time. This is important and needs to be taken seriously. The American people need leadership and results. The current President won't do this, but if the Republicans engage in this level of transparency and faithfully do it in a dynamic way, promoting not only information but with some charisma, then the American people may pay attention and maybe learn about conservative principles. Again, the goal is not fiddling around and appearing reactionary. The goal is to teach conservatism, provide accountability and clearly contrast what bills, legislation and action Republicans are taking and how Democrats are not being responsive to *Cut, Cap, Reform and Balance.* The American People are smart. Getting Americans the information is the hardest part, but one that can be won, if enough initiative is put into it.

Supreme Court Appointees

The President's selection of Supreme Court Judges is also important. Some may say it is more important than anything else. A lot of women may be interested in the selection process because the Left has made them fearful that the Right is going to do everything it can to over-turn Roe versus Wade. The President is sworn to an Oath to execute faithfully the duties of the Presidency and uphold the Constitution. Supreme Court Judges are to fully embrace the Constitution. The judges cannot be ones who think the Constitution needs to be revised or rewritten. There are many judges out there who think the Constitution is a living document and thereby needs to be altered to adjust with the times. While we can amend the Constitution to reflect changes, there is a process put in place by our Founders. However, the body and frame work of the Constitution is not to be altered. Judges who have a position contradicting the Constitution cannot be faithfully recommended to uphold the very document they seek to destroy. It is not about putting a liberal judge on the bench versus a conservative. It is about putting a judge on the bench who believes in and upholds the Constitution of the United States of America.

It is a scary time in American history because we have two Supreme Court Justices who may retire within the next four years. Under the current Administration it is assumed the appointee will be liberal and reflect the opposite of conservative principles. It is in this area the Republicans need to hold the line and insure the confirmation hearings and related processes are held to the highest standards. There is no room for judges on the Supreme Court, who do not embrace and support the United States Constitution. Their support of the Constitution is reflected in their writings and decisions rendered. There can be zero ground given in this area.

The American people need to be reminded of this prior to one of the judges retiring. The media and President Obama will clash with the Republicans over this and make it an issue. The key is to make it an issue now, on Republican terms, so the people are already prepared and understand the backdrop. Waiting until a crisis or decision has to be made is lose/lose for Republicans. Take the fight to the Democrats before the crisis and keep it in front of them throughout. Be aggressive, assertive and proactive by being solution-focused.

Passing Bills through the House

I am not sure where this fits in within the book. It could easily have gone in an earlier section, but I think it needs to stand out. I don't know how this process works or what it is based on, but it needs to change. For example, the House can pass a bill, but the Senate does not have to pick it up and vote on it. It may work the same way from the Senate side of things when they send Bills to the House. Also, the Senate has not passed a budget in three or more years. How can that stand?

The most shocking piece of this process is how Ear Marks make their way into Bills that really don't have a lot to do with the specific Bill being voted on. A Bill needs to be one to three pages in length and be only about the Bill being voted on. I don't know how it got complicated or this difficult, but it needs to stop. There doesn't need to be Add-On(s) in the Bill for extra spending in order to get a politician to vote in favor of it. The Bill either passes or it doesn't on the merit of what is being presented and the politicians need to have the integrity and character to vote up or down based on the Bill. How many times have we, the people, heard about extra spending in a Bill that has little to do with initial proposal? I hear scuttle implying that is how it is done if the Bill is to be passed. That is crap and needs to change.

The Line Item Veto has long been pursued by the Executive Branch to cross through areas of spending in a Bill. The Supreme Court struck this down in 1998 or so and though President George W. Bush attempted to get it reviewed again, it died somewhere along the way. The problem is not the President in this case. However, due to the lack of leadership in the White House, it may not be good for the President to have the authority to strike through items he or she does not want in a Bill if that means he or she could then sign it into law without review from those who sent it initially to the White House.

Our representatives in both Houses need to learn how to present a Bill with integrity. Republicans can add some integrity to the process by introducing a Bill on how a Bill is to be introduced and how it to flow through the Houses. It is silly to think that we need a Bill to introduce a Bill, but again, when other people are spending other people's money, no one really cares...and it shows. Republicans can change this image and it can help them with the American public who perceive most politicians as being dirty and immoral.

Chapter 9
American Family Values

"The First Amendment of the Constitution was not written to protect the people of this country from religious values; it was written to protect religious values from government tyranny"

Ronald Reagan, 1983

Parenting

The American family is not on trial. The American family has already been sentenced and those still believing in traditional values need to fight hard for the appeal. We need to have a come to Jesus moment in our society. The average parent spends very little time with their child in active engagement. This is not acceptable by any measure and most likely will not change. The American family values have changed. The American culture reflects selfishness and behaves like a two year old wanting what he or she wants, when he or she wants it and throwing a tantrum when being told "no." Parenting is hard. Parenting is challenging and it can sap the life out of you sometimes. Anything worth achieving comes with a price. If parents are not actively involved with their kids someone else will be.

As a therapist, I can assure you I frequently meet with kids whose parents do not spend / invest time with them. In most cases, kids I meet with do not know their father and their relationship with their mother are strained. The most important "product" adults develop in their lifetime is developing their children. Values, beliefs, ideals and character come from relationships. The American family is broken. Praying together, eating together, playing together, being together is not the norm, but the exception. We do what we can to drive a wedge between us and family. We have heard of the war on poverty. We have heard of the war on drugs. We have heard of the war on illiteracy. If you want to know where the real fight is in our country it is at home.

Each of the wars mentioned were heavily financed but to no avail. Why? The key is family. Listen to kids who faced struggle and hardship and achieved great things. Most report their mother and/or father demanded more from them and would not let them settle for less. Behind every successful person was a parent or relative who pushed that adult when they were young. The concept you have to work for what you get is losing its meaning in our current world. There are a high percentage of individuals who have been lured into believing they don't have to rise up and achieve, but they can just settle and have the basics handed to them. This mentality starts first in the home. It starts first with the inconsistent interaction of parents with their children. It starts first with reinforcing to kids everywhere that everyone's effort is equal and that there is no established standard to rise up to because we are all different and therefore achievement is in the eyes of the beholder.

I hear people, especially other therapists; indicate there is no correct way to raise children. These people state parents just need to do the best they can and hope for the best. While I agree there are no guarantees for anyone, there are foundational blocks needed to improve chances of a successful outcome. These principles involve: active involvement, communication, consistency and structure, fairness, accountability, values training, work ethic, instilling the joy of learning, goal setting, responsibility, modeling and discipline. Parents have to put the work into parenting, into training and coaching their kids to, not only enjoy life, but to go for the brass ring and reach their dreams. Instead, we are raising kids who are learning to settle and have lowered expectations, rather than teaching each to rise up to the challenge.

When I speak with parents, many don't seem to understand family time and togetherness. There seems instead to be a collection of individuals residing in a home or shelter as oppose to developing core family relationships and values. Parents spending time with their kids without television, IPADs, phones or rushing to get to the next place seems foreign. Parents with less means are also caught up with similar distractions. When was the last time you played with your kids or enjoyed time with your family? When, was the last time, emphasis was placed on being home and doing things together? It is too easy to divide up and meet out somewhere or to be on the go all the time. Most parents know this is not good for the family and yet don't change, because "that's how parenting is today." Well, I have news, parenting by today's standard isn't working all that well and children are proof. Parents need to rise up.

I could write another book on fathers and call it *Fatherless Nation*. The number of children who don't have two traditional parents in their home is staggering. Men, abandoning their responsibility as fathers, is one of the big reasons why adolescent crime is on the rise. Go to any big city having lots of crime, like Chicago, and I will bet there is direct correlation between the percent of crimes committed and those not having a father in their life. I have the utmost respect for single parents, whether it is the mom or the dad, but there is a reason it takes a male and female to conceive a child. It is not just biology. It takes two raising children because it requires the perspectives of both genders and the hard work of two people. Marriage is not old fashion, which typically means out of date, but it does require work, as does parenting, as does anything worthwhile. This is missing in our society.

The growing expectation in families is becoming "We want what we want and we want it now." We don't appear to understand how instant gratification has grafted itself to our morrow and infected our spirit and mind. We see having things as being rights and going without as being criminal. When some put up roadblocks to this kind of thinking, these same people are accused of being old fashion. We are losing our way as a people and as a nation and there are no politically correct responses to it. Rather than accepting the raw truth and calling it what it is, we dismiss it and continue to do the same thing hoping it will work.

We have become distracted as a people and have placed priorities on things rather than people. We, the American family need to fight hard. We need to decide on the values we want to raise ourselves and our kids with and how these values are connected to our country. These American values are connected to our founding. These values reflect our beliefs. Too often I meet with parents who are well intentioned individuals, but don't know what he or she is doing. Their goal is to show up each day and do the best they can with their kids and hope it works. They lack intentionality, focus, and discipline. Our families will never survive this way. Businesses won't survive this way. America won't survive this way. Rise up parents and demand more from yourselves and expect more of your kids.

Education

Education is a great example. I don't know what the figure is, but I imagine the

United States spends more money on education than any other country in the world. Throwing money at a problem is never the answer. The big issue with education is the lack of value placed on it at home. Parents expect the schools to teach their kids. Somehow the responsibility for the child to learn has shifted to the school system. Whose kid is it? Parents are responsible for teaching and educating their child. Skill training, teaching, character building, goal setting, academics, and how to behave in society are the core functions of parenting. Somehow we have given this responsibility to the schools, to the government and kids are failing because of it.

The schools in our country are trying to teach combative and disruptive kids who really don't need to be there until their parents teach each how to behave and instill in each the desire to learn. Remember, I have worked with difficult children and adolescents all my adult life and I have profound empathy for each and their background. While each need a chance to succeed and display their gifts as individuals, each need to rise to expectations, rather than having expectations lowered and their behavior excused. This is an injustice to them and it enables kids and their families to remain irresponsible.

Adults who have earned a college degree are less likely to live in poverty and to be unemployed. The same is true for married couples. Current social programs reward the opposite. Most programs assist those not married and those without education. The benefits go away once an individual achieves. Individuals get used to the financial support and determine it is better to live on the support. America is creating a welfare state and the Democrats are bordering on buying votes to maintain their power. After all, those relying on the financial support from the government are not going to vote for those wanting to reform these programs.

Parents need to be about challenging their kids through having high expectations for them. Parents also need to be teaching their kids about the opportunities in this country and how to lessen the obstacles while their children pursue their dreams. Parents who demonstrate this proactive approach to their children and teach their children how to improve, even beyond the parent's achievements, lays a great foundation. Education comes down to three pillars: values, principles and beliefs. Parenting comes down to the same. Ultimately, when these three pillars are discussed one has a tendency to run into the God topic. This is where things get a little dicey in this book. I certainly don't mean disrespect to those who may be offended, but values, beliefs and principles stem from having a solid foundation.

In God We Trust

The idea that there is separation between Church and State is too vague to be considered so black and white. It is kind of like the verse in the Bible that says, "God helps those who help themselves." It doesn't exist anywhere in the Bible, but a lot of people quote it as if it is there. Our founders were mostly individuals of faith. Our country was founded on Judeo-Christian values, principles and beliefs. Did our founders want separation with Church and State? Yes. Remember, in that time period, the Catholic Church was a part of the Ruling Class. Our founders desired to create a land where all could worship freely or not at all. They envisioned a country where people were not persecuted because of their faith or their right not to believe in God. This was an amazing vision and one our country wants to honor and uphold.

While the founders wanted the people to be free, they did not strike God from the core values of America. "In God We Trust" is on our currency. George Washington put his hand on the Bible when he was sworn in. This is a tradition most presidents follow today. Remember, it was the Democrats during their convention that eliminated God from their platform (Good, 2012). They added God back days later and in the process received booing from their own crowd (Tapper, 2012). God through the Christian faith is woven throughout our history. While forced allegiance and worship is not America's goal, it is foolish to think our country is separate and apart from Judeo-Christian values. "I do solemnly swear to tell the truth, the whole truth, so help me God" is a common phrase declared by a witness in a court of law. It is often done with a hand on the Bible.

Conservatives are often blamed for wanting to legislate based on morality. How can you have laws without laws being based on morality? Who decides and what is it based on? In America, we historically take our cues from Judeo-Christian principles. Approximately 78% of Americans (Newport, 2009) consider themselves to be Christian, that is, to believe in Jesus. A lot of America's founders were Christian (not all) and our country is rooted in these principles. Laws are not separate from morality. There is no real defense for stating that stealing is against the law without having a value or belief that stealing is wrong. What tells us stealing is wrong is not universal thought, but beliefs rooted in religion.

Over the next hundred years America needs to be careful. We have become full of ourselves in how we view freedom. Being able to do whatever we want whenever we want is chaos. True freedom is promoted through inward discipline and structure. Discipline and structure imposed externally ends in anarchy. It is almost like the people want to be ruled in some way because they have so far gone off the track, they can't do it themselves. Liberals want to rule. Liberal theology is about putting all in a box because people cannot govern themselves successfully.

I am not suggesting oppression of rights in any way. I am not saying we need to serve a particular religion. That was actually struck down years ago by our representatives and rightly so. There are many Agnostics and those who worship other religions that are alright with the traditions of America when it comes to Christianity. I have friends who are Agnostic who get caught up in the Christmas festivities. What makes America unique is the ability to worship freely in this country without persecution or government interference. However, this is changing and in the effort to be politically correct, America is allowing the few, who have an axe to grind about Judeo-Christian beliefs, to infringe upon our traditions and rituals.

As a social worker, I certainly understand the power the majority possesses in this country and how it impacts those in the minority. While this is important, America was founded on certain principles, values and beliefs. We can't separate out our government from this without tearing the very structure of what America stands for down with it. From a layman's perspective, countries are similar to being in a club. Every club has a creed, by-laws, mission statement and constitution. If a person likes the club, they join and accept what the club is about and if the person does not want to join or does not want to be in the club anymore, than he or she discontinues their membership.

Perhaps a club analogy is not the best example. Consider living in North Carolina and being a collegiate basketball fan. For men's basketball there are two dominant teams that have a strong rivalry with one another: The University of North Carolina at Chapel Hill (UNC) and Duke University. If a student attends UNC and is a Duke fan that individual can still be a Duke fan. He or she can still promote Duke, cheer for Duke, wear Duke clothing and while at games, cheer for Duke all he or she wants. The individual has a right to exercise her ability to free speech. She may get booed or encounter resistance but he or she can pull for Duke as long as it is done responsibly.

However, the Duke fan is going to have zero luck changing the culture of UNC. While UNC will respect the Duke fan's opinion to a point, UNC is not going to change the culture of the campus to promote anything other than school pride in being a Carolina Tar heel. UNC will not have an all inclusive day at sporting events encouraging their fans to wear the opposing team's logo or cheer for the opposing team. They want the other school to know that on the UNC campus, being a Tar Heel is their number one priority. It is done responsibly, but it is done to promote the way of life of those who call UNC their school. It is what UNC and, for that matter, every other school across the country is about. The Duke fan doesn't have to be a UNC fan while attending school, but he or she does have to accept the values, traditions and rituals of what it means to attend UNC.

America, like all other countries has a constitution and being a citizen means the individual accepts the values, rituals, traditions of America. You can accept without agreeing and the great thing about being in America is the government cannot force you to be involved in the values, rituals and traditions. The problem I have is those who work so hard to present a case on how America's values, rituals and traditions need to be discontinued because they are offensive. These individuals have a right to free speech and can voice this, but society does not need to be held hostage. If an individual feels that strongly about how hideous and offensive America is then there are other places in the world to live.

Does it mean that all have to believe and buy into what America stands for? No. Does it mean that the principles America were founded on will force all to believe the same thing? No. Does it mean that people are free to voice their opposition to these values and protest as they see fit? Yes. Does it mean that people can choose to worship their own faith or choose not to worship or believe it all? Yes. It also means America does not have to bow down to political correctness and give in to all this madness from those who oppose American values and traditions. America is a Judeo-Christian nation that traditionally believes in the Deity of God, namely Jesus. America culture is inseparable from these core beliefs and to be passive about what it means to be an American is detrimental to our ability to thrive as a country.

Consider the Jewish population in America. America loves the Jewish people because Jesus was Jewish. Have you ever wondered why America stands with Israel? It is not just the relationship we have had with Israel since it reappeared on the map in 1948. It goes much deeper. Scripture in the Bible references God's blessing on the nation that stands with Israel (Genesis 12:3). Our traditions and values run deep in Judeo-Christian beliefs and there is no getting around it. America is a collection of people who believe in freedom and the individual. America elects representatives to be their voice in government and to lead based on these values outlined in our Constitution. You can't separate America from these values and beliefs. It is who we are as a nation.

There is a movement in our country wanting to break all ties with our Christian beliefs and how these beliefs are involved in our government. We have seen this with taking prayer out of our public schools (Hallowell, 2012). Some places have been forced to remove references of the Ten Commandments from their court houses (Fournier, 2011). Every Christmas season we see people verbalizing their frustration with how Christmas offends them and there are active efforts to interrupt Christmas holiday celebrations (O'Reilly, 2012). There are plenty of examples growing in the belly of America that are coming forth and will come out even more over the next fifty to one hundred years.

Jews and Christians need to really examine how voting for the Democrat Party aligns with their respective beliefs. No, I am not saying voting Democrat means you aren't religious or even Christian. It was the Democrat Party who removed God from their platform at the 2012 Democratic convention. It was at the same convention that the Democrats also removed Jerusalem as the recognized capital of Israel. It was the Democrats who mandated religious institutions provide for reproductive health care needs that contradict their spiritual beliefs. We can go down the list, but it is compelling. I won't fall prey to being identified as some lunatic on the right making idiotic statements. I am simply saying that a lot of the beliefs represented in the Democrat Party are not necessarily rooted in Judeo-Christian values, beliefs and principles.

America stands only if the values for which it stands for, "One nation, Under God.

With Liberty and Justice for All," are embraced by the masses, not because all believe in it, but all embrace it for what it means to live in America. We need to be careful as Americans. We can't please everyone and we can't apologize for who America is as a whole. We have a fantastic history. There have been dark periods of gross misconduct and cruelty. There has also been great vision at a time, when the rest of the world was rooted authoritarian rule. Yes, the founders needed to end slavery at the time of America's founding. No, there is no excuse for them not doing so. However, at least the America they founded provided the frame work to free people and allow for the individual, rather than the rule of government. America stands for freedom. Freedom is not the same as doing whatever an individual wants. True freedom derives from structure, discipline and accountability. The Left goes too far in big government development and Libertarians tend to go too far to the Right with minimal to no accountability. Rules, laws, oversight is healthy. Regulation is not evil. Conservatism strikes the balance (not to be misunderstood as a republican moderate) and is proven to work.

We need to stand together now more than ever. We need to remember our history and what it means to be an American. We need to teach our history at home with our children. We need to raise our children reflecting the values, beliefs and principles promoting what it means to be an American. While our kids are a part of a larger world society, our kids are Americans first and our kids need to know what being American is all about from their families. Being American is about liberty, excellence, perseverance and all the other characteristics we have discussed in the previous pages. It is about loving your country and honoring those who have fought for our freedom. The American family needs to rise up and take responsibility back for raising their children by putting the time, sweat and discipline into coaching, teaching, cheering, training their children. America has always been about the family. Rise up America and look at what is being taught to your children. Ask yourself, does this propel my child to reach his or her potential? Does this promote individual responsibility? Does this reflect the core values I want, as a parent, for my child to live by until he or she can decide otherwise? Family is the key to a healthy foundation. Children really are any society's future. Right now, America's future is suspect. A society has to have a common core of principles, values, traditions and rituals that binds it together. Rise up America. When our backs are against the wall we stand with one another. We need to always remember who America is.

Chapter 10
Home of the Brave

"Character, not circumstances, makes the man...Character is power"
Booker T. Washington

Teach Conservatism

Conservatism in this country has a great chance at showcasing to the rest of America and to the world why conservatism works and how it works for all. Conservatism needs to be taught and we need brave individuals to rise up and teach. Conservatism has to answer questions in order to set the record straight. One primary issue with conservatism and the economic approach put forth by the Democrats is on the issue of the economy. Over the last 96 years, Republicans have held the White House for 48 years and the Democrats for 44 years. In that time frame, the Democrats have created more jobs than Republican presidents. Conservatives can't argue it. The numbers support the claim.

The answer, of course, is related to all branches of government. The House, which holds the purse strings, has long been dominated by Democrat rule. It is seldom the Republicans who have the majority in Congress, let alone both Houses. When Republicans have held both Houses, like Republicans did in 1994, and you have a President like President Clinton who agrees to work in a bipartisan manner, than great economic growth occurs. When the President and the Houses are divided, then a lot of effort has to go into building relationships and forging a partnership for the good of the country. Ronald Reagan did that with House Speaker Tipp O'Neal. President Obama has not done that with House Speaker John Boehner.

There are those who will offer endless suppositions on why their approach to government works and why we need to change to this or that to keep up with the times. Think back to the founding of this country. The intent was freedom from government rule. In that day, people were subservient to the governing body. The government was authoritarian rule of the King. People only had the rights the King told them they had. The people existed for the purpose of the King and his designees. There were no real rights for the commoner. The commoner was to live as if he was lucky to have breath and to stay out of the way of the ruling class.

I am not saying that all Democrats are liberals and that all liberals are socialists and so on. I am certainly not saying all Republicans are conservatives. I am not saying that there aren't valid points to what Democrat presidents have done for the good of America as well as those who have served in all areas of government. What I am saying is that the ideology of government caring for its people by deciding what they need or don't needed is succinctly opposed to the principles this country were founded on. America is founded on less government. America is founded on individual liberty. America is for the individual to own government rather than being owned by government. Government is to serve the people not the other way around. Some ideas on the function of government are as follows:

- Protect its citizens from foreign and domestic threats
- Protect the rights of its citizens and uphold the Constitution
- Balance the budget on an annual basis / spending 20% of GDP
- Reduce national debt (35% of GDP)
- Create accountability and regulations that protect citizens, but don't hamstring businesses, so effective economic growth occurs
- Growth is measured by: 10 million private sector jobs need to be the minimum bench mark for any president per term (trending up as population increases)
- Federal employees are less than 1.5% of the total US citizen population including military personnel
- Measure full time employment, rather than unemployment numbers that are often manipulated

We are the greatest country in the world. I don't know that I have the solutions. I have written many times in this book that I am not an economist and have never held public office. If we are going to tax wages, then I do know all who work, need to pay taxes. Most Americans agree. All, who don't work, need to pay taxes, like the proposed national sales tax. The United States federal government does not have a revenue problem. The United States federal government has a spending problem. The federal government revenue is tied up in its tax code problem. If you make it low enough so everyone pays and make it affordable to pay, so people keep more of their money, then it lessens the burden and shares the responsibility. Again, I love this country and pray for its leaders. There are many holes and many issues with my proposals. I am not married to the numbers I propose. The percentages may need to be adjusted. I don't know if my math adds up, but what is scarier is the reality that the politicians can't do math at all. It would be great and speak of my brilliant mind if I was on the money, but I may have laid an egg. The goal here is to stimulate real conversation towards real solutions.

Our politicians have hit a wall or, better said, "The" wall. Nothing is getting done. They need to change. Behavior needs to change. We want results. We want performance. We want a strong work ethic. Each of them needs to remember, they work for us. They can talk about the free ride many get in this country and they would be right. However, politicians getting a free ride need to end too. You can't please everyone and you can't care for everyone. Decisions need to be made and priorities need to be set.

Presidential Leadership

The President is to lead. He or she cannot do everything and although the buck stops at the president's desk, he or she cannot insure there will be no problems, scandals, disasters, crises and/or wars. Problems and issues come up. It is why we need a leader. To be a leader, one has to lead. We need a President, who says to both Houses, "I will build a relationship with you and work with you. We will meet weekly or however is appropriate. I will come to you. You will come to me. We will roll up our sleeves, stay up all night and do what it takes to map out a workable plan, inspiring growth and confidence in the American economy.

The art of leadership is not just making decisions. It is not telling people what to do. It is not just being in the position of leadership. Leadership is earning the respect of those you are leading. Those following evaluate a leader based on the leader's behavior. Integrity, work ethics, decision making, support, relationship building, expression of ideas, embracing ideas, delegation, taking charge; all of this is wrapped up in behavior and is evaluated closely by others. America needs leadership and its thirst for it will not be quenched until the leader leads like an American. The American leader needs to get our house in order financially and he or she can't do it by dividing. It has to come from uniting and lifting others up.

Analogy on America's Condition

I conclude with another analogy in regards to America's current state of being. Imagine you are in accident and you are bedridden in a hospital for three months, as you recover from your injury. The doctor informs you that you are now ready for physical therapy to learn how to walk / move again. The prognosis is straightforward. If you work hard and follow the medical team's recommendations, you will make a full recovery. You question the phrase "full recovery," but you are relieved you have some form of hope. The doctor concludes by emphasizing, if you don't work hard, and choose instead to become dependent on the supports you have now due to your injury, your current condition may become irreversible. You look at the doctor and acknowledge your understanding.

You start off physical therapy and it is hard, painful and you don't want to keep doing it. You look around the rehab room and see people who are similar to you. There are those in full body braces and many with miscellaneous contraptions assisting them regain their mobility...their life. You see people who have lost limbs and adjusting to prosthetics. You notice the man, who obviously lost mobility due to fire and is fighting everyday to get his movement back. Each day you put off working hard in physical therapy you take a step towards codependency. Each day you go to physical therapy and work hard, you take a step towards independence and reclaiming your life and abilities. You have times when you "feel" good about your progress and days when you can't go on. Along the way you see others give up and those who won't quit. You see those who do well enough to leave and those whose hope is dashed by complications. You despise your situation and yet you fight because you want to get out. You don't understand people you have seen who have a real shot at full recovery, but instead settled for their current life. You feel for those who would like to press on, but can't. You encourage those who are struggling while you continue to fight for recovery. You let go of those who have the ability, but who have given up, wanting instead to be cared for and propped up, while dismissing the medical teams report that full recovery is in their grasp. You rationalize that you just don't have energy to invest in those who are not investing in themselves. Right or wrong, you move on, focused on getting better. Each day you have a decision to make. You make the choice to fight, to reclaim your life.

Like this analogy, Americans have to decide what America is to be. The choice is ours.

Do American policies propel people to unlock their unique gifts to achieve great things? Have American policies in some ways become a crutch, that while the policy intended good things, its real impact on people is containment through contentment? Are they pushing people to strive to get back on their feet or be satisfied with the status quo? The goal of social programming needs to be a safety net that is time limited and challenges individuals (those having the ability and the appropriate prognosis) to reclaim their life. It doesn't need to be complicated. As Americans, we will always strive to help one another. That has never been in question. What we Americans need to have a problem with, all of us, is creating a system where people lose sight of their God-Given right for something more because they have settled for the scraps falling from the government table. Don't let that be you.

America is the individual, not the masses or the collective. You were designed for an extraordinary purpose. You have gifts no one else has and you are unique in what you offer this country. The flip side is true too. While we are special, we are also expendable. We can choose to waste our gifts and talents or develop them. The great thing about this country is it is truly up to us. We decide. We can do or be anything we want to be because the "American Dream" is purposely woven within the very definition of America. This is not true in all parts of the world. This "Dream" is being threatened and over the next century America has a big test. Do we remain committed to our core beliefs in individual liberty, the Constitution and capitalism or do we fall prey to a cradle-to-grave "nanny" state that promotes irresponsibility. Great societies have come and gone over the years. If America is to survive, if

America is to thrive, if America is to lead, then the people, who are America, need to rise up. Protest peacefully. Rise up at the voter box. The best predictor of future behavior is past behavior. Over the last 50 years we have seen a shift in America that leans to propping the individual up, rather than promoting liberty. Demand more from YOU and from those we elect. The elected officials work for us. We send them to their positions to serve us, the people. They are to promote liberty and the core values of this country. They work for us, the individual. We own this country. Who is America? You are. Who is America? I am. Who is America? We are. Rise Up America.

Sources

The following references are general and site sources off the Internet unless otherwise named. While the author has made every effort to provide accurate source addresses, etc. the author does not assume responsibility of changes to websites or errors related to sites. The sites referenced do not necessarily reflect my values or beliefs.

Archer, B. (1998). Welfare Reform's Unprecedented Success. http://www.washingtonpost.com/wp-srv/politics/special/welfare/stories/0p081098.htm

Arrillaga, P. (2012). The Huffington Post: 'War on Women' 2012: Amid Controversy, Women Ponder How They Became Campaign Issue. http://www.huffingtonpost.com/2012/05/12/war-on-women-2012_n_1511785.html

Banschick, M. (2012). Psychology Today: The Intelligent Divorce: How to get yourself and your kids through a break-up. http://www.psychologytoday.com/blog/the-intelligent-divorce/201202/the-high-failure-rate-second-and-third-marriages

Blodget, H. (2012). Business Insider Politics: Yes, This Chart Showing That Most Debt Growth Came Under Republican Presidents Is Accurate, But... http://www.businessinsider.com/who-increased-the-debt-2012-9

Boyle, M. (2012). The Daily Caller: Nanny state report: NC school officials reject preschooler's homemade lunch. http://dailycaller.com/2012/02/14/nanny-state-report-nc-school-officials-confiscate-preschoolers-homemade-lunch/

Bradford, H. (2012). Bush-Era Tax cuts Will Cost US Nearly $1 Trillion Over Next Decade. http://www.huffingtonpost.com/2012/08/24/bush-era-tax-cuts-revenue-expire_n_1828657.html

Braveheart. The Movie. (1995).

Brouhard, R. (2011). About.Com: First Aid. How to Rescue a Drowning Victim. http://firstaid.about.com/od/drowing/ht/07_drowning.htm

Censky, A. (2012). CNN Money: Audit the Fed? Bernanke fights back against Ron Paul.
http://money.cnn.com/2012/07/18/news/economy/fed-bernanke-ron-paul/index.htm

Coal News: Coal's Foremost Publication. (2011).
http://www.coalnews.net/facts.php

Cooper, A. & Brackman, H. (2009). US News: The Threat of the Human Shield Strategy Hamas Uses Extends Beyond Israel, Gaza.
http://www.usnews.com/opinion/articles/2009/01/09/the-threat-of-the-human-shield-strategy-hamas-uses-extends-beyond-israel-gaza

Cox, J. (2012). Record 46 Million Americans on Food Stamps.
http://www.cnbc.com/id/48898378/Record_46_Million_Americans_Are_on_Food_Stamps

Davis, L. (2012). Fox News: Two Bill Clinton legacies that Obama should not ignore.
http://www.foxnews.com/opinion/2012/09/05/two-legacies-from-bill-clinton-that-obama-must-not-ignore/

Day, D. (2005). The Space Review: Boldly Going: Star Trek & Spaceflight.
http://www.thespacereview.com/article/506/1

Doherty, D. (2012). Town Hall: Busted: Obama Says He Never Called Anyone "Unpatriotic"
http://townhall.com/tipsheet/danieldoherty/2012/09/19/busted_obama_says_he_never_called_anyone_unpatriotic

Dwyer, R. (2010). DWYER: Bush Tax Cuts Boosted Federal Revenue.
http://www.washingtontimes.com/news/2010/feb/3/bush-tax-cuts-boosted-federal-revenue/

Edwards, C. (2009). Agricultural Subsidies.
http://www.downsizinggovernment.org/agriculture/subsidies

Encyclopedia Britannica. (2012).
http://www.britannica.com/EBchecked/topic/498842/Republican-Party

Fax, B. (2011). Forbes: The Problem with Supply-Side Economics.
http://www.forbes.com/sites/billflax/2011/02/10/the-problem-with-supply-side-economics/

Ferrara, P. (2011). Forbes: Reaganomics Vs. Obamanomics: Facts and Figures.
http://www.forbes.com/sites/peterferrara/2011/05/05/reaganomics-vs-obamanomics-facts-and-figures/

Francescani, C. (2012). NY Mayor Blasts Sugar Ban
Critics: "That's a lot of soda".
http://www.reuters.com/article/2012/06/01/us-usa-
sugarban-newyork-idUSBRE85012N20120601

Frequently Asked Questions on Gift Taxes.
http://www.irs.gov/Businesses/Small-Businesses-&-Self-
Employed/Frequently-Asked-Questions-on-Gift-Taxes

Foster, J.D. (2008). The Heritage Foundation: Tax Cuts,
Not the Clinton Tax Hike, Produced the 1990s Boom.
http://www.heritage.org/research/reports/2008/03/tax-
cuts-not-the-clinton-tax-hike-produced-the-1990s-boom

Fournier, D. (2011). Catholic Online: Federal Court
Orders Ten Commandments Removed From Florida
Courthouse.
http://www.catholic.org/national/national_story.php?id=
42127

GasPriceWatch.com.
http://www.gaspricewatch.com/web_gas_taxes.php

Greenhouse, S. (1991). The New York Times: Half of
Egypt's #20.2 Billion Debt Being Forgiven By US & Allies.
http://www.nytimes.com/1991/05/27/business/half-of-
egypt-s-20.2-billion-debt-being-forgiven-by-us-and-
allies.html

Good, C. (2012). ABC NEWS: Democrats Shift Language on Israel, Remove 'God-Given' From Platform. http://abcnews.go.com/blogs/politics/2012/09/democrats-shift-language-on-israel-remove-god-given-from-platform/

Griffin, J. & Housley, A. (2012). Fox News: Military TimeLine from Night of Benghazi Attack Begs More Questions. http://www.foxnews.com/politics/2012/11/11/military-timeline-from-night-benghazi-attack-begs-more-questions/

Hallowell, B. (2012): Today Marks the 50th Anniversary of the Prayer Ban in Public Schools (& Here's the History). http://www.theblaze.com/stories/today-marks-the-50th-anniversary-of-the-prayer-ban-in-public-schools-heres-the-history/

Hancock, TJ. (2011). Housing Bubble, Financial Crisis – What Happened, Who is Responsible. http://tjhancock.wordpress.com/housing-bubble-financial-crisis-detailed-comprehensive-assessment/

Hannity, S. (2011). Fox News: Perry Claims He Can Secure the Border in One Year as President. http://www.foxnews.com/on-air/hannity/2011/11/03/perry-claims-he-can-secure-border-one-year-president

Hayes, C. (2012). this is What 'Saudi America' Looks Like.
http://tv.msnbc.com/2012/12/08/this-is-what-saudi-america-looks-like/

Holy Bible. Genesis Chapter 12, verse 3.
http://www.biblegateway.com/passage/?search=Genesis+12%3A3&version=NIV

Isidore, C. (2012). CNN Money: Japan Owns Almost As Much US Debt As China.
http://www.thestreet.com/story/11600851/1/kass-foul-play.html

Jaffe, M. (2011). ABC News: Senate Shoots Down Controversial Ryan Budget & President Obama's Plan, Too.
http://abcnews.go.com/blogs/politics/2011/05/senate-shoots-down-controversial-ryan-budget-president-obamas-plan-too/

Jeffrey, T. (2012). CNS News: Obama on Pace to Borrow $6.2T in One Term—More Than All Presidents from Washington Through Clinton Combined. http://cnsnews.com/news/article/obama-pace-borrow-62t-one-term-more-all-presidents-washington-through-clinton-combined

Kang, C. (2011). The Washington Post: Nine of 10 teenagers have witnessed bullying on social networks, study finds. http://articles.washingtonpost.com/2011-11-09/business/35282386_1_social-networks-social-media-amanda-lenhart

Kass, D. (2012). The Street: Kass: Foul Play. http://www.thestreet.com/story/11600851/1/kass-foul-play.html

Keynesian Economics. http://www.econlib.org ; http://www.econlib.org/library/Enc/KeynesianEconomics.html.

Kurtzleben, D. (2012). http://www.usnews.com/news/articles/2012/01/17/gingrichs-uncomfortable-facts-about-food-stamps-hold-water

Leno, J. (2012). The Tonight Show on NBC. http://www.nbc.com/the-tonight-show/video/dennis-miller-part-2-82712/1414926/#

Lewis, J. (2011). The Day The Suffrage Battle Was Won.
http://womenshistory.about.com/od/suffrage1900/a/aug
ust_26_wed.htm

Lewis, R. (2011). The Robin Report: "Keep your friends
closer and your enemies closer" The Godfather Strategy.
No confirmation Sun-Tzu made this statement
http://therobinreport.com/keep-your-friends-close-and-
your-enemies-closer/

Lieb, D. (2012). The Huffington Post: Todd Akin
'Legitimate Rape' Comments Remain Focus of Missouri
Senate Race.
http://www.huffingtonpost.com/2012/10/25/todd-akin-
senate_n_2015666.html

Longley, R. Small Business Drives U.S. Economy.
http://usgovinfo.about.com/od/smallbusiness/a/sbadrive
s.htm

MacDonald, E. (2012). Government Workers Earn More
Than Their Private-Sector Counterparts.
http://www.foxbusiness.com/politics/2012/01/31/govern
ment-workers-earns-more-than-private-sector/

Madison, L. (2012). CBS News: Richard Murdock: Even Pregnancy From Rape Something "God Intended." http://www.cbsnews.com/8301-250_162-57538757/richard-mourdock-even-pregnancy-from-rape-something-god-intended/

Miller, SA. (2012). New York Post: Down to brass tax: Rate hikes, entitle cuts in fiscal cliff compromise. http://www.nypost.com/p/news/national/down_to_brass_tax_Nbw5JQ6XRqTj0Od0JF2EPK

Moffett, D. (2012). About.com: Immigration Issues: Newt Gingrich on Immigration. Former House Speaker Backs More Moderate Policy Than Most Republican Rivals. http://immigration.about.com/od/immigrationlawandpolicy/a/Newt-Gingrich-On-Immigration.htm

Moskowitz, Clara. (2012). Space.Com: Apollo Moon Landing Flags Still Standing, Photo Reveal. http://www.space.com/16798-american-flags-moon-apollo-photos.html

The National Black Republican Association: http://suwanneegop.com/NBRA%20Civil%20Rights%20Newsletter-2.pdf

Nation, S. (2012). Shallow Nation: President Obama: Univ. of Colorado Boulder Campaign Speech Video: Sept. 2, 2012 Norlin Quad.
http://www.shallownation.com/2012/09/01/president-obama-univ-of-colorado-boulder-campaign-speech-video-sept-2-2012-norlin-quad/

Newport, F. (2009). Gallop Polls: This Christmas, 78% of Americans Identify as Christian

http://www.gallup.com/poll/124793/This-Christmas-78-Americans-Identify-Christian.aspx

Norquist, G. (2011). The New York Times. Read My Lips: No New Taxes.
http://www.nytimes.com/2011/07/22/opinion/22Norquist.html

Noyes, R. (2012). Fox News: Five ways the mainstream media tipped the scales in favor of Obama.
http://www.foxnews.com/opinion/2012/11/07/five-ways-mainstream-media-tipped-scales-in-favor-obama/

O'Reilly, B. (2012). The O'Reilly Factor: Bishop E. W. Jackson.
http://video.foxnews.com/v/1940243549001/voting-democrat-is-bad-for-african-americans/

O'Reilly, B. (2012). The O'Reilly Factor: The War on Christmas: The Big Picture. http://www.foxnews.com/on-air/oreilly/2012/11/30/bill-oreilly-war-christmas-big-picture

Paul, R. (2011). Fox News. Ron Paul: Offensive War is Un-American! Close All US Military Bases Around the World! http://www.ronpaul.com/2011-06-22/ron-paul-offensive-war-is-un-american-close-all-u-s-military-bases-around-the-world/

Reagan, R. (1981). Inaugural Address. http://www.reagan.utexas.edu/archives/speeches/1981/12081a.htm

Ritz, E. (2012). The Blaze: US Near Deal To Forgive #1 Billion in Egypt Debt: 'Its's About Growth & Business.' http://www.theblaze.com/stories/u-s-to-forgive-1-billion-in-egypt-debt-it%E2%80%99s-about-growth-and-business/

Rotherham, A. (2007). Conservatives and No Child Left Behind. http://www.npr.org/templates/story/story.php?storyId=9434814

Sahadi, J. (2009). 47% Will Pay No Federal Income Tax. http://money.cnn.com/2009/09/30/pf/taxes/who_pays_taxes/index.htm

Self-Employment Tax (Social Security and Medicare Taxes). http://www.irs.gov/Businesses/Small-Businesses-&-Self-Employed/Self-Employment-Tax-(Social-Security-and-Medicare-Taxes)

Snopes. (2010). http://www.snopes.com/politics/religion/capital.asp

Smith, A. (1904). *Wealth of Nations*. London: Methuen & Co, Ltd.

Sperry, P. (2001). The Heritage Foundation: The Real Reagan Economic Record: Responsible and Successful Fiscal Policy. http://www.heritage.org/research/reports/2001/03/the-real-reagan-economic-record

Tapper, J. (2012). ABC NEWS: Demos Quickly Switch to Include "God," "Jerusalem." http://abcnews.go.com/Politics/OTUS/democrats-rapidly-revise-platform-include-god/story?id=17164108

Thatcher, M. (2011). *Margret Thatcher In Her Own Words*. London: Biteback Publishing.

Understanding Supply Side Economics. http://www.investopedia.com/articles/05/011805

Wall, K. (2012). News-Leader: Statistics reveal stark challenges for children raised in one-parent households.

http://www.news-leader.com/article/20121125/NEWS01/311250054/Statistics-reveal-stark-challenges-children-raised-one-parent-households

Wardrop, M. (2009). The Telegraph: 'Tough Love' parenting gives children a better start in life, study finds. http://www.telegraph.co.uk/health/children_shealth/6524954/Tough-love-parenting-gives-children-a-better-start-in-life-study-finds.html

Webster On-Line Dictionary. http://websters-online-dictionary.org/definition/entitlement

Wehner, P. (2011). Commentary Magazine: Barack Obama, Political Hack. http://www.commentarymagazine.com/2011/12/08/barack-obama-political-hack/

Williams, R. (2011). The Numbers: What are the federal government's sources of revenue? http://www.taxpolicycenter.org/briefing-book/background/numbers/revenue.cfm

Worstall, T. (2012). Why The Fair Tax Will Fail. http://www.forbes.com/sites/timworstall/2012/08/22/why-the-fair-tax-will-fail/

Wright, C. (2012). The Washington Post: Stacey Dash Supports Mitt Romney, Gets Racial Backlash on Twitter: Not All Blacks Must Be Democrats.
http://www.washingtonpost.com/blogs/therootdc/post/stacey-dash-supports-mitt-romney-gets-racial-backlash-on-twitter-not-all-blacks-must-be-democrats/2012/10/09/22f792b6-1229-11e2-be82-c3411b7680a9_blog.html

Wunder, W. (2010). The US Supreme Court, in 1895, ruled unconstitutional a federal law containing income taxes, with arguments concerning class warfare and the definition of a direct tax.
http://suite101.com/article/income-tax-declared-unconstitutional-a208974

Chapter 11
After the Credits Roll

"Reconnecting Americans to what is true leadership, what it looks like, smells like and how to recognize it when it is present is the very essence of America's founding. Perhaps the closes we can come in this day and age to its rediscovery is through cinema. Is it any wonder why we, as people, cocoon ourselves in these storybook realities? God help us."

Robert Lindsay, 2013

After the Credits Roll Talking Point

Conservative messaging comes in many ways and not just from politicians. The real conservatives out there, who have real pull and influence, need to meet with high powered, name-brand names in Hollywood, maybe like Clint Eastwood, who would consider producing a television show to reconnect Americans to conservative principles. The 2000s had The West Wing. There needs to be a conservative counter to showcase what real conservative values and leadership is and how conservative principles promote individual responsibility and the Constitution of the United States.

Television Show Theme of Executive Decision

The show is called *Executive Decision* (based on novel). It is about strong leadership and involves tracking down bad guys, who wish to do Americans harm, cleaning up the corruption in Washington and promoting solutions to restore America to greatness. The President for the starring role either has to be an actor, who is a conservative or an actor who is willing to depict a conservative. I am thinking someone like Tom Selleck, Mark Harmon, or Dennis Haysbert. It has to be someone who conveys strength and decisiveness. Of the three, Haysbert has a deep commanding voice and a presence that resonates with people (*while I have suggested actors to play certain roles in the following pages it by no means indicates these actors are conservative or reflect any of the philosophy laid out in this book or for this proposed television series. It simply means I am a fan of their work and think they are gifted at their craft. Any inference that any or all would play a character or subscribe to conservative values is unintended*). The President in this role has to be characterized and portrayed by the actor as a man of honor and integrity. His immediate cabinet and key personnel need to be individuals with no moral drama or flaws when it comes to doing their jobs. Each can have their own quirks and deficits, but not in the area of honor and integrity.

If you have seen the shows *24* or *The Unit* then you know the level of action and suspense television can provide. **Executive Decision** can have these elements to provide suspense, moral dilemmas and opportunities for support characters to sacrifice their values, beliefs and principles. However, there can also be a lot of drama in addition to all the suspense and action to provide a back drop on how government is to function. **Executive Decision** demonstrates how to collaborate and balance things out, so power hungry individuals don't compromise the core values making up America. It can teach how a Bill is to be drafted and presented and expose the flaws in the process as it is done today. It can expose the political double-speak, cover ups, and all the other elements associated with federal government politics. The Director of the series or movies can throw in the corrupt, the endless amount of compromise and adultery that transpires, along with the greed that strangles the once principled-centered politician who was going to change the world. The goal of the show is to teach and reconnect the American people with conservative values, beliefs and principles. The show, through great writing, needs to showcase these principles and how conservatism benefits the individual as well as the country. The acting will take care of itself if there is good writing and editing.

Background on Executive Decision Plot

Odin Cross (suggested portrayal by Dennis Haysbert) has just been elected the 45th President of the United States. He is a man of principle and integrity. Though forces may come against him, he and his inner-circle, never deviate from their values. There is plenty of intrigue and scandal with others to choose from, but the main characters act as one. Cross and his administration are charged with addressing the 9.8 unemployment rate, the reckless federal spending, the 1.3 economic growth rate of the country, 59 million people on Food Stamps, 1 out of 3 on some type of federal assistance and the 20 trillion dollar national debt. China is passing the United States as the world's largest economy in late 2016. The Chinese Yuan has steadily moved up to 9th in the world and is scheduled to become the world's currency in 2024. Gasoline at the pump is $5.95 a gallon and the national health care law is having the opposite impact those who initially supported it had hoped it would have for Americans. The branches of government have been at a stand-still, and now, in 2016, the people finally woke up and voted the Republicans majority in the House and Senate in addition to the Presidency.

What does Cross do? How will he lead? How will he temper the Republicans, who are too eager to change everything because they are in charge? How will he lead those in the Republican Party who are power hungry and just as corrupt as those they charge the other side as being, but can't see it in themselves? Cross knows he has to work with all politicians and not blackball the opposition. Cross understands opposition is the balance of government. Cross believes he has to win people by showing how conservatism can positively impact society and the good of all if implemented correctly. He is passionate about his principles and those who are learning who he is see that he is not the average politician. Cross is different and he scares the hell out of both sides. Meanwhile, the people appear to love him.

Season One, Episode One

President Odin Cross starts out the episode in deep dialogue with a budgetary team about going line by line through the federal budget to identify all areas of spending and what the specific purpose is for each expense. He is in his fourth month of his presidency and he made a commitment to personally go through the federal budget within the first six months of his presidency to determine where all the money goes and why. After the research he wants to begin working on his 2017 budget proposal based on what he has discovered. He wants to conduct a lot of research and then work on getting the two political parties to review it before it is voted on in March of 2017. The budgetary team is stumped by the amount of detail Cross wants and he begins to speak into their hearts by teaching them about proper planning versus going through the motions. He uses references of planning out in detail how military operations are prepared for or what business have to do to understand where their expenditures go. His sleeves are rolled up and the viewer gets the impression he is heavily involved and not just delegating this job to subordinates.

His rationale is the American people need to have fiscal responsibility originating in the White House. His mantra is *Protect, Cut, Cap, Reform and Balance.* The scene opens up with him and his team pouring over various aspects of the budget as if they had been there for hours. There are some that are grumbling about effective ways to spend their time and Cross has to address their loss of focus on his agenda. These are not necessarily his key players, but individuals identified to assist him understand how programs are allocated and for what purpose beyond the black and white. The setting is the White House in the Oval Office. The viewer is able to grasp that Cross is driven by his commitment to America and not someone to be played or conned.

The moment of enlightenment for his team is interrupted when a call comes in through Watch Command that the American Embassy in New Delhi, India has been attacked and those inside are fighting off the aggressors. Cross knows Secretary of State, Ben Fusao (suggested portrayal by Ken Watanabe) and his delegation are inside meeting with the Chinese and the Russians about a way to get the Arabic community to stand up against terrorism. Cross immediately summons his secretary to get the Secretary of Defense on the phone. He also clears the meeting he was once engrossed in, while his secretary gets in touch with all the appropriate members for the pending briefing on the Embassy attack. The key personnel are being assembled in the Oval Office and emphasis is placed on how President Cross leads and how he collaborates with his team in an effort to build a framework of trust and confidence in one another.

Characters (suggested actors/actresses to portrayal role)

Odin Cross is 54 years old, a businessman turned politician, and served in the Navy for twenty-two years. He married young and had kids young. His wife, Nadia (suggested portrayal by Stacey Dash) have a daughter and a son who are both in their thirties now and do not play an active role on the show. Cross became a SEAL and then finished his career as a SEAL Commander. It was during that time that he became Commander of a young, promising SEAL, Jason Garrett (suggested portrayal by Kiefer Sutherland, Max Martini, Aaron Eckhart or Mark Valley) who is now the Commander of SEAL TEAM SIX which specializes in various types of missions including counter terrorist operations. Cross trusts Garrett as much as he trusts Nadia and this trust is never compromised. He considers putting Garrett on standby as he and the Defense Secretary, Susan Davis (played by Lynda Carter or Sela Ward) decide the options and how to collaborate with all the foreign powers involved. The season doesn't stay stuck on rescuing the Secretary of

State and the other hostages. This is accomplished within four or five episodes. The real task is tracking who sent them and taking them out of operation.

Odin Cross went from high school to the Navy. He used the military to get his degree in Business Administration. While he was attending University of Virginia he met Nadia, who was in school to be a counselor. They bonded and got married within the year. He became a father at the age of twenty-three. After he retired from the military at the age of forty, he started an on-line company providing individuals/companies with computer back up for their computer files and virus/firewall protection. He started this company in 1999 just before the attacks on September 11, 2001. He became very successful and earned a lot of money and eventually sold the company for 210 million dollars. He also had the instincts to invest heavily in Apple when their stock hit rock bottom and made a fortune off them and other investments. His estimated worth is 250 million. In 2012 he became disenchanted with the direction of the country and ran for Governor of North Carolina and won. He was successful and decided to run for President in 2016 and won by a six percent margin. He is not a career politician, but he is passionate about wanting to fix the screw ups of all parties, so the American people can pursue their dreams. He has no axe to grind, no angle to push. He is open-minded to all schools of thought, but the one thing he can't stand is deception and he won't compromise on the founding principles of America.

Nadia is four years younger than he and although she had to stop her studies to become a parent and raise her children, she later returned and earned her degree and then her master degree in counseling. Nadia shares her husband's views on America and was an active supporter of his military career. She knows Garrett, Cyndi and Bill well. She is a source of strength for Odin and she is the one who steadies him behind the scenes. While Odin does not put up fronts or act a part, he does believe he has to convey strength and resolve to this team and to the people, but with Nadia, he can play, relax and not have to have any answers. Nadia knows her husband's struggle with anxiety and feelings of inadequacy which is why he works out so much. He refers to Moses being a reluctant leader. The martial arts, boxing and intense fitness training helps him take the edge off and reminds him of days when life was simpler. She also knows Garrett would give him a hard time if he let himself go too much. His prayer life is rich and he relies on God. He can struggle with her and he is safe. She likes this side of him because it is their secret moment where he communicates how much he needs her. No one else can listen to him like Nadia.

Nadia Cross is known around the White House as someone who is pleasant and treats all, the help included, like they have been friends for life. She knows names and birthdays and is someone people just want to be around. She reflects approachability and is considered a fragrance for life in a place that life is often strangled. She is highly capable and intelligent and displays confidence when speaking to others. She is the ultimate First Lady and embraces the role. Her advice is often sought after by those in the White House about their personal issues and struggles. People just feel like they can confide in her, but she is unmistakably clear that if it involves the country or something her husband needs to know she will share it with him. She keeps personal disclosures to herself and sees it as her role to use her skills as a therapist to help others. She is shrewd and not easily manipulated. Her helping others never gets in the way of anything connected to Odin's presidency. Again, no one messes with her or even thinks to because of the bond she has with her husband. She has great influence with Odin and he never discounts her advice.

Secretary of State, Ben Fuaso, is Japanese-American. His parents emigrated from Japan before he was born. He is a man of measure, intellect and is known for his ability to bring people together to solve problems. His Zen-like presence promotes peace and harmony and his level headed decision making makes him perfect for his new position. Like Cross, Randal and Davis, Fuaso has private sector experience and knows how to work deals. He is man of ethics and though he does not know Cross like the others do, he respects his ability to lead, agrees with the conservative ideals to promote change in America and is looking forward to being on his team. Cross has taken a special interest in Fuaso because he is one of the few that is close to him that he does not know well and wants to make sure he feels he is an intricate part of the team. Cross is pissed this has happened so early into their relationship together and considers Fuaso's captivity personal above and beyond the rage he feels for the attack levied against America by terrorists. Ben's wife, Mia (suggested portrayal by Patti Yasutake) and their three adult children are immediately provided protection beyond what they were receiving. Nadia makes it her task to get to know Mia and treat the Fuaso's like family. This is a great comfort to Mia who is scared for her husband. She wants to trust Cross, but she doesn't know him and he can't tell her anything. Mia feels in the dark and Nadia eases the pain of not knowing.

Jason Garrett is the Commander of SEAL TEAM SIX and served under Commander Odin Cross. Cross and Garrett became like brothers and their wives hit it off too. Garrett has developed into an extraordinary leader with great success. Jason leads like he was trained, with integrity and grit. He has no use for those who are not carrying their weight and sees the life of each of his teammates as being his number one priority in any mission. He doesn't take unnecessary chances and does not rush into combat on faulty information. If he feels set up or used as a guinea pig he will seek out the rat and expose him or her. Jason is loyal to his new Commander and Chief. Jason is the most elite soldier Cross has ever seen. He is an expert at hand-to-hand combat and ranks superior in all related testing. He doesn't just use brawn, but thinks through problems as a brilliant strategist. They know each other well.

Garrett also was bullied by peers in elementary school, physically abused by his father before his mother kicked him out of their lives. He was also sexually abused when he was 11 years old by a neighbor before he and his mom moved. Odin and Nadia know his life story. He has a tender heart for kids and when he is not on missions, he and Cyndi volunteer at the local schools and teach students how to build an environment where bullying is not tolerated. While Garrett is sensitive to being pushed in a corner, he has the ability to compartmentalize his job and his past does not impact his ability to execute his missions. If anything, it gives him approachability to the steely presence he projects. It is Cross and Garrett who are the main stars of the show. They will forge a partnership to track terrorists and others just as evil and deal with them. He has the direct number of the President and Cross has instructed his staff that if Commander Garrett calls they are to interrupt him. Commander Garrett is to have direct access to the President whenever Commander Garrett thinks it is important.

Jason has a wife, Cyndi Garrett, but they were unable to have children. Cyndi (suggested portrayal by Christina Applegate, Alyssa Milano, Mary Stuart Masterson or Catherine McCormack) at times is resentful of her husband's job, but she is supportive and they are best friends. She is good friends with Nadia Cross. In fact, the four of them have been close for years and consider the other to be family. Cyndi finds great comfort in her friendship with Odin and Nadia, especially when Jason is away. She can stand on her own two feet and knows how to take care of herself. She got a job as Realtor, dabbling in the field to keep her mind busy while Jason was away. She eventually launched her own real estate company in 2003 and enjoyed great success despite the housing market crash. They live on a 25 acre farm in Brown Summit, North Carolina that was given to them by Cyndi's grandparents. The Cross's own 500 acres right down the road.

Defense Secretary, Susan Davis (suggested portrayal by Holly Hunter, Lynda Carter or Sela Ward), is 56 years young, attractive, and yet strong. She served in the Navy for twenty years on various ships. She and Cross had met a few times when she was Commander of amphibious crafts dropping him and his Team into harm's way, but there are no sexual overtones. He is loyal to his wife and she is loyal to her husband, who was also in the Navy. She has two grown children as well and though they are not on the show she is close to them. She is also one of the few women to see combat behind enemy lines without the public knowing about it. She used the military to pay for school where she got a degree in Business Administration and Marketing. When she retired from the military with the rank of Commander she and her husband started their own security business. She provided high price security for diplomats, world leaders, stars and the like. She has connections everywhere and like Cross, she is not one to be pushed.

The Chief of Staff, Bill Randal (suggested portrayal by Dennis Miller) is a longtime friend of Cross and is able to speak to him in ways others don't dare. He is a truth teller and does not mix words. People think him to be arrogant because of his vocabulary and how he comes across, but he is actually compassionate. Cross knows his friend well and trusts him to have his backside. Randal earned his law degree from Stanford. He was married and had two kids, thirteen and seventeen when they were killed in an airplane crash in 2005. He blames himself for not being on the plane with them. He was a litigator and specialized in criminal law. He was in the middle of a trial that his wife told him not to take, but he refused to listen to her because of the high profile case. The guy was dirty, but he didn't care at the time.

After his family perished in the crash, Randal came to the end of his rope and wanted to die. He quit practicing law. He had planned to blow his brains out six months after his family died, when out of the blue, Odin and Nadia came by his house to check on him. Odin took the gun out of his hands. He moved in with Odin and Nadia for a few months until he recovered. When Odin ran for Governor, Odin wanted Bill to handle the campaign. The same with the presidential race and now, as Chief of Staff, he is entrusted with protecting his friend and his President. He drinks alcohol a little more than he should, but is not considered an alcoholic, at least by him. He can back off the bourbon when necessary, but will admit he finds comfort in a few drinks. He enjoys impromptu conversations with Nadia, who provides him therapy to deal with his demons whether he wants it or not. He doesn't have a family anymore and considers the Cross family his own. He lives at the White House and there are times that Odin may shoulder his slightly tipsy friend to his room and tuck him in. Randal is single and has no interest in having another family. He credits Cross with giving him purpose again and will not allow anyone to hurt him while at the same time, not violating the integrity of how Cross wants to lead.

The National Security Advisor, Jena Malcom (suggested portrayal by Madeleine Stowe, Demi Moore or Ally Walker) holds a

PhD in Political Science. She also was involved in the Peace Corp and is fluent in Spanish, Russian and Chinese. She is highly intelligent and a great strategist who can identify areas of need or concern quickly. She is an effective planner and is strong willed. This is not a deficit as it tends to come across for most females in film. She is a hard worker and wants to do a good job and she wants her people to do a good job. She respects Cross and met him through his wife, Nadia, many years ago. She has few friends and does not interact well with others. The Cross's accept her for who she is and Nadia became her friend. There is some awkwardness on her part to know how to be social and she knows this about herself which is why she throws herself into her work. There are times during briefings when she has heard what she needs to hear and she just walks out and goes to work. Some are offended at her lack of presidential etiquette, but Cross finds it humorous and lets Malcolm be Malcolm. She is single, but sees men regularly. She has no interest in children, but values her own mother and the role a mother plays in an individual's life. She is always in control, never compromised and enjoys companionship that is brief.

White House Press Secretary, Jill Slotski is 41 years old and (suggested portrayal by Ana Torv, Catherine Bell, or Poppy Montgomery) was a Liberal in her college days. Over the course of the last Administration she began to see these policies as being unfulfilling. She began to do her own homework on conservatism and came to the conclusion American best works on a capitalistic approach rooted in conservative principles. Since she was heavily involved in protesting the Bush Administration she was quickly sought after by a cable new station to be a contributor for their news network. She embraced this role and made a lot of inroads with the Democrat machine. She was completely on board with

President Obama until the end of his first four year term. She then began questioning everything and researching the impact of liberal policies on job growth and the good of the American people. She came to the end of herself when she realized she doesn't practice these concepts in her personal life.

Jill has her own demons to work through. Matters of faith are dear to her heart, but she can't forgive herself for past mistakes. While in college she had a boyfriend and got pregnant. She didn't want a baby and got an abortion without telling him or anyone else. They broke up and after graduating, she met the man of her dreams. They got married and then she discovered he was a nightmare. He tried to control her and became abusive. They divorced. Two years later she married again. They had a good marriage or so she thought. They tried to have a baby, but discovered he was sterile. They discussed adoption, but he did not want to adopt and felt like a failure for not being able to help his wife get pregnant. He began drinking a lot and she poured herself into her career. They divorced on amicable terms, but both left empty and wondering if God had anything good for them out there.

She was tired and looking for something else to give her meaning in her life and had decided that she was on her way out of politics when she met Cross. She became intrigued by what made him different. She began to cover him and ask really hard questions. He had answers and appreciated her tenacity. When he was elected, Cross and Bill met with Jill and shared Cross's vision for the country with her and asked her to come on board to be Press Secretary. She relished the opportunity and valued their confidence in her. She is unflappable, conveying insight about what the Administration is doing for the American people, and yet, displays command over the Press Corp room by not putting up with any junk from reporters wanting to make a name for him or herself. However, if the reporter is reputable and is seeking the truth, then she has time and patience for this level of questioning. She knows the media's game and Cross was clear to her that her role was to share conservatism and encourage others to do their homework as she had. Her role is to inform the American people. Her role was to be the mouthpiece of the Administration. If at any time she felt she was being misled by the Administration she was to come to Cross directly. The goal was and is integrity, but based on need to know.

Central Intelligence Agency Director (CIA), Constance Santiago is 48 years old, and (suggested portrayal by Benjamin Brad) goes by Connie. He initially signed up with the Marines and transferred to the CIA due to his ability to be obscure and as a linguistic expert. He served as a Field Operative for years and knows Garrett well. He climbed the ladder before retiring from active service. He became involved with

Davis and her security firm and served as her Operations Director. When Cross won the presidential election, Santiago was immediately tapped to replace the terminated CIA Director. The Senate confirmed Santiago making him the youngest to ever serve at that post.

Santiago is divorced with a teenage son he never sees. It bothers him and he does not know how to approach him. His son would love to have a relationship with him, but is angry that his dad chose to serve his country over him and his mother. His mother never bad-mouths his dad, but the two just never had a real chance to spend time together and work the marriage through. She packed up and left and returned to Colorado which is where she is from and has now remarried. Santiago sends notes to his son, keeps a journal for him in case he dies and keeps an eye on him from a distance. He can infiltrate any place in the world, confront violent extremists and speak with confidence about assets and related counter measures, but he stresses over speaking to his son and feels he trips over himself when they do speak. He feels inadequate as a father and believes this inadequacy is rightly deserved.

Conrad James, US Attorney General, (suggested portrayal by Chi McBride) is a friend of Bill Randal. They went to law school together and though they drifted apart, Bill has respect for him. James has a great legal mind and a sarcastic tone. He and Bill differ often and their interactions spark the comedy relief on the show. They both have good comeback lines to the other's remarks. The viewer gets the impression these two have faced off one too many times in the court room. When it comes down to business though, Conrad is knowledgeable, insightful and can be temperamental. He has a wife and three children who are still in primary school. He is a good father and husband. He is loyal to Odin because Bill vouched for him, but there is a hint of Conrad watching Odin's decision making to see if he truly is a man of honor. Although Bill and Conrad are good friends, Conrad does not know about Bill's attempt to end his life. No one does except Odin and Nadia and that is the way it stays. Conrad knows just about everything else about Bill and is not afraid to bring it up to Bill. They have fun with one another and are good at breaking down how the judicial system was intended to work versus how it currently works.

Conrad does not have any deep emotional scars in his personal life. He served as lead Prosecuting Attorney in New Orleans before becoming District Attorney. He has regrets over cases that were lost due to faulty evidence, police work or poor legal representation. He loves America. He loves the Constitution and is considered an expert on the founder's intent of the Constitution. He has a great work ethic. He considers himself neither a Republican nor a Democrat and is registered as an Independent. When asked by Bill Randal,

"Who did you vote for?" Conrad responds, "None of your damn business." He is trying to clean up the mess from previous Administrations. His interactions with Malcolm, the National Security Advisor, are interesting because of her quirks and his quick wit. Odin likes him and values his input.

Anyone Cross brings into his inner-circle the viewer can bet he or she is battle-tested and has character. This is a show about unity, integrity and doing what is best for America. It is about leading with conviction in a city where there is only corruption. It is about taking pride in your country's leaders and relating to the difficult decisions that have to be made. Again, the scandal and hook-ups that are infamous for television and movies can still be there. Viewers enjoy those well-timed hated characters that inflict emotional torment on others. Where this show is different is the core cast knows how to recognize these individuals and deal with them. America needs to see leaders lead and stand up for principle, rather than always seeing those beloved characters fall prey to some stupid form of blackmail or love triangle.

Purpose of the Executive Decision

How will Cross be consistent in these situations, despite distractions, so he can take care of those in harm's way? How will he lead? How will he aggressively expose and fix the corruption in Washington and thereby restore America's confidence in those elected? How will he protect the Homeland? Who will write the narrative and more importantly than all the above, what will he, the President of the United States, do in the moment of decision, to exemplify what it means to be Commander and Chief.

The show will also tackle, by being fair, the journalistic responsibility of the press to hold government accountable. No Administration is perfect and government that is so large, it is impossible to know what everyone is doing all the time. Journalists play a key role in asking the tough questions and investigating those in power to keep all in check for the good of the American people. The series is about action, suspense and drama. The show bounces from the field of battle or conflict to the world of policy and deception. It focuses on Garrett and Cross tackling national security issues. It also shows the legal side of policy making and the impact it has as it filters to the states and local communities. It addresses immigration reform and growing the economy. It reflects on the Constitution and the intent of our founders. It addresses the evolution of the Republican and Democrat Parties. It identifies corruption and those who are corruptible. It has deceit and an espionage element. It takes on health care, frivolous spending and the PORK aspect of Bills generated in the Houses. The show, if done correctly, has the opportunity to entertain and inform the public about how conservatism promotes individual responsibility, ingenuity and allows for a free society. It can contrast conservatism with socialism, liberalism and others. It raises the question; can a person lead America and remain a person of honor and integrity? Is there anyone behind the scenes who thinks he gets to pull the strings of those in charge? It shows mistakes being made and those responsible taking ownership and contrasting it with those who assign blame – on both sides of the aisle. It also showcases peace through strength with decisive decision making to protect our citizens and support our troops, while not seeking to jump into every war out there.

It is perfect for the FOX network, but could be interesting on HBO, Cinemax, Netflix, or any number of channels. Contact Eastwood, Jerry Bruckheimer, Jack Welch, Roger Ailes, Donald Bellisario or someone else with influence because until then, it is just words on a page. It can be great entertainment that will capture viewership and sponsors. This author would want to be involved in said project (novel series to in the works) to insure there is integrity with the concept. RISE UP!

Pay It Forward

Youth Unlimited is a non-profit organization located in High Point, North Carolina that has been serving at risk children, teenagers and their families since 1968. The agency is small, but provides quality treatment to those it serves. While Youth Unlimited serves families on Medicaid there are many families who seek help, who are not on governmental assistance and have private insurance, which does not cover these enhanced services. These families have fewer options than those on governmental assistance. Help Youth Unlimited serve all in need and not just those on social programming by joining their financial team of supporters. Visit Youth Unlimited website: www.youthunlimited.cc

Give an annual gift of $9, $17, $25 or any other amount ($9.00 is the equivalent of one movie ticket or one cheap dinner out on the town or 2.5 gallons of gasoline for your car).

Give one time annually. Get one friend to do the same. Have him or her to do the same, and so on. By getting just one person to give as you do and that person getting someone and so on, it is not beyond the imagination to hope for as many as 300,000 individuals giving $9.00 or more annually. This domino effect will allow Youth Unlimited to reach its goal and get off governmental assistance, so the agency can provide services to those desiring help, regardless of their socio-economical background.

All financial contributions are tax deductible

Youth Unlimited has not read or endorsed the ideas in this author's book. The author's intent is to help a local agency broaden its financial base in an effort to help those needing assistance in the surrounding area.